Reinvent Yourself

Psychological insights that will transform your work life

Susan Kahn

KoganPage

First published in Great Britain and the United States in 2024 by Kogan Page Limited

2nd Floor, 45 Gee Street
London
EC1V 3RS
United Kingdom

8 W 38th Street, Suite 902
New York, NY 10018
USA

4737/23 Ansari Road
Daryaganj
New Delhi 110002
India

www.koganpage.com

Kogan Page books are printed on paper from sustainable forests.

ISBNs
Hardback   978 1 3986 1331 7
Paperback   978 1 3986 1329 4
Ebook   978 1 3986 1330 0

British Library Cataloguing-in-Publication Data
A CIP record for this book is available from the British Library.

Library of Congress Control Number
2023951196

Typeset by Integra Software Services, Pondicherry
Print production managed by Jellyfish
Printed and bound by CPI Group (UK) Ltd, Croydon, CR0 4YY

Praise for *Reinvent Yourself*

'Dr Susan Kahn has that rare ability of being able to communicate complex ideas into accessible, practical applications. She encourages us to never give up hope, to connect, to reconnect and re-emerge, chrysalis-like, to face the world anew. Truly a book for our times.' ANDREAS LIEFOOGHE, FOUNDER, OPERATION CENTAUR

'An invaluable tool for those considering a change in career or just wanting the opportunity to reinvent themselves.' ZOE SINCLAIR, CO-FOUNDER, THIS CAN HAPPEN

'An inspiring guide for planning – and believing in – meaningful change.' SHAHROO IZADI, BEHAVIOURAL CHANGE SPECIALIST AND AUTHOR OF *THE KINDNESS METHOD*

'Offers energy, excitement and heartwarming inspiration to anyone interested in learning from those whose life path has taken a twist or turn they did not expect, or necessarily choose.' RACHEL ELLISON MBE, LEADERSHIP COACH AND AUTHOR

'Highly recommend for anyone wanting to take a well-considered approach to planning their career.' NATALIE LANCER, CHAIR, BRITISH PSYCHOLOGICAL SOCIETY'S DIVISION OF COACHING PSYCHOLOGY

'Beautifully balances the theory with the practical, the honest with the hopeful, and the need to find acceptance with the need to find courage. This book brings together a range of different perspectives and tools to help reinventors navigate this often-messy process and, most importantly, invites them to find self-compassion and look inside for answers.' PAULINE MCNULTY, CO-FOUNDER, PLAYFILLED

'The insights are thoroughly grounded in psychological theory and philosophy, but the practical nature of the book and the wonderful examples make it both entertaining and genuinely useful.' RAUL APARICI, COACH, FACILITATOR AND HEAD OF FACULTY, THE SCHOOL OF LIFE

'Completely resonates with the current times. A warm and encouraging approach underpinned by depth of experience and research that shines through.' NICOLA GRANT, FOUNDER, SHE2 LEADERSHIP

'I love Susan Kahn's work. The way she blends social science and personal insight makes her work readable and valuable in equal measure, as this book shows.' DANIEL FINKELSTEIN OBE, JOURNALIST AND AUTHOR OF *HITLER, STALIN, MUM AND DAD*

For those who are stuck, you can reinvent yourself

By the same author

Death and the City: On loss, mourning
and melancholia at work
Bounce Back: How to fail fast and be resilient at work

Contents

List of exercises

About the author

Dr Susan Kahn CPsychol is a business psychologist, speaker and academic. She is a chartered psychologist and coaching psychologist with the British Psychological Society (BPS) and a Fellow of the Association of Business Psychologists (ABP).

She works as an executive coach, consultant, mediator and an observer of working life. She has a particular interest in the behaviour of people at work and below the surface dynamics in organizations.

She has taught coaching psychology at Birkbeck, University of London, for a decade and developed the Master's programme in 2019. She is a faculty member at the School of Life, working with businesses to help them learn, heal and grow. She also works as a group relations consultant. Her research interests embrace leadership, coaching, change and vulnerability at work. She is a board member of This Can Happen, empowering workplace mental health.

www.drskahn.com

Foreword

This is a book that believes in you and your capacity to reinvent yourself.

It offers psychological theory in easy-to-digest language, with guidance and ideas that will transform your work life. Throughout the book are practical exercises that will allow you to apply your learning, reimagine new perspectives and get a deeper understanding of the many psychological ideas that Khan explores.

Peppered throughout are numerous reinvention stories from the world of politics, fashion, sport and music – stories that illustrate the potential we all have to change, to reinvent.

It explores the way we view the world, the changing nature of work and the joys of an uncertain future. From planning to neuroplasticity, from the self-limiting beliefs we associate with our age to the need for self-efficacy. From leader to follower, from stuck to unstuck – Kahn takes you on a journey of discovery and possibility.

I loved it and I challenge anyone not to take something new and something practical to use in your daily life.

Imagine a conversation on a comfy sofa with a trusted confidante, someone who wants the best for you but is willing to tell you some hard truths.

That is *Reinvent Yourself.*

Nicola Mendelsohn CBE
Head of Global Business Group
Meta

Acknowledgements

Writing this book has been a joy and pleasure, interesting and challenging but also a lot of work. As the late great Jonathan Sacks said, no great achiever, even those who made it seem easy, ever succeeded without hard work. While I would not describe myself in those terms, I am aware of the privilege of being able to write and the support that has surrounded me. My tribe has grown since the last book was published but the sentiment remains: I would take a bullet for you. Thank you my beloved Neville, Tori, Oliver, Charlie, Francesca, Sam and our treasured Teia and Poppy. A special mention for Sylvia Kahn who has reinvented herself with courage.

Gratitude to my critical readers: Suzanne Ellis-Ferera, Anna Levy and Oliver Tenzer, and those who have helped me think: Dr Jenny van Heerden, Dr Anton Obholzer, Dr Maya Shankar, Shankar Vedantam, Professor Andreas Liefooghe and Professor Adam Grant. And my constant, Judi Newman.

Matt James has been a wonderful editor, challenging and generous, wise and insightful – my appreciation extends to you and to Kogan Page.

A heartfelt thank you to all those whose reinvention stories have featured, especially those who spent time with me. Your capacity to change and reinvent has been inspiring:

Anita Banerje, Arielle Steele, Edward Enninful, Elizabeth Smart, Eugene Choi, Florence Kennedy, Hillary Rodham Clinton, Jake Arnold, Jake Daniels, Jason Ardey, Jeremy Newman, Jo Elvin, Joe Winch, John McCormack, Karen Wagner, Kate Davies CBE, Liz O'Riordan, Lucy Kellaway, Mark Stringer, Maya Shankar, Michael Rosen, Munroe Bergdorf, Nicholas James, Nick Vujicic, Raphael Rowe, Ryan Arthur, Sheryl Lee Ralph, Stormzy, Tara Swart, Victoria Beckham, Volodymyr Zelensky and Zak Abel.

Introduction

This book is about reinvention; about how we all have numerous opportunities to rethink who we are, how we work and what we have to offer the world. We can think about change and development in many ways. This book uses psychology and the multiple insights and techniques on offer to support transition.

Psychology can help us to move from one phase to another; it can help us to understand ourselves and others better; it can help us to become more aware of the systems in which we live and work. In short, psychological insights can support us as we navigate the cycle of work life with its inescapable endings and beginnings.

We all experience touchpoints in our lives – moments when we rethink, question or are forced to examine the way we are living and working. At times those touchpoints are externally imposed – we are made redundant, we suffer loss, we are injured or, as the world experienced, a global pandemic directs us to act and work differently. These moments are a challenge to us; we have a choice to welcome the opportunity for growth and development, or to deny these changes and resist the inevitable transformations we are facing.

There are also numerous occasions when our response and reaction to events has some connection to external events, but a dominant connection to the forces within us, our beliefs about who we are and what we are capable of, the possibilities open to us and the attitude we bring to the experiences we encounter. At times these beliefs can be enhancing and encouraging, giving us courage and delight, but often our beliefs are self-limiting. They can box us in and prevent us from trying, leading us to regret and missed opportunities.

I should state from the outset a bias to the possible and declare the belief that we can rewire our thinking, that we can revitalize. I believe you have the potential to change. This might not be easy and may require considerable effort, some good fortune, and a shift in mindset, but this book will accompany you as you regenerate and refresh your belief in your power to reinvent yourself.

In shining a light on reinvention, I am conscious of the potential reader who is considering the subject because they do not value themselves. They see their contribution to the world as less than and feel the need to do more, be more, achieve more. These ambitions are congruent with what is on offer, but I would like to emphasize that wherever you are now, whatever it is you have done, whatever you have accomplished thus far is OK. You are enough, but you are choosing to rethink and to evolve.

How to use this book

This book is divided into sections that you can navigate in a linear fashion, or you can dip into each chapter that calls to you. The way the book is organized reflects the way we connect with work. Our path through our working life is not straightforward and different challenges and options occur in unexpected ways.

So the book has been written to allow you to explore the area that seems most interesting to you – perhaps you prefer to go from start to finish in an organized way, or perhaps you will find one area of particular interest, and that is where you dive in.

What is consistent is that each chapter features insights from psychology, from attachment theory and identity work to trauma and vulnerability, from neuroscience and psychotherapy to somatic understanding and stoicism. Each chapter draws on particular psychological concepts and then highlights one or more case studies of individuals who have experienced reinvention, showing how psychology can help us to understand their transformation.

Throughout the book you will read reinvention stories: the CEO who retired and then returned a year later; the journalist who became a teacher; the dyslexic model who became the editor of *Vogue*; the veteran who became a mental health campaigner; and the comic actor who became a globally admired leader, as well as the many who reinvented their working lives post the pandemic.

Not all reinvention stories are about glory. Sometimes it is about acceptance and temporary landings. Nor do all transformations have joyful outcomes: there are founders who become destroyers, those who achieve their dreams only to realize that the dream was not theirs but one imposed on them by family and society, that the fantasy of their new working identity was just that, and the reality a deep disappointment.

This book will guide you to greater understanding of your own transformations, through an in-depth exploration of your values, an opportunity for greater self-awareness and a chance to re-evaluate the decisions you have taken. In short, you will be able to change the way you embrace opportunity, with thought and consideration given to your motivation and reward.

Each chapter ends with some practical exercises and tips to allow you to draw on the theory and apply it to your own experience of reinvention and change. In essence, this is a toolkit for your own reinvention.

I have long been fascinated by our capacity for reinvention. In my work as a business psychologist and coach I am often sitting at the boundary of an organization, observing teams and leaders, with a perspective that gives insight into their changing behaviours and growing confidence. In my academic and teaching life (I work with mature and experienced students), I witness the evolution of career identities and am hugely motivated by people's capacity to learn, reflect and reinvent. Building on my research into resilience and what allows us to bounce back from failure and catastrophe, my exploration of reinvention is a natural progression.

It is often quoted that all research is 'me' search. That in our endeavours to find out more about patterns of behaviour, theory and thinking, we are revealing much about ourselves. Reinvention is a topic that means a lot to me personally, and therefore this book is a heartfelt exploration based on my own deep belief in the power of reinvention built on greater understanding and self-awareness.

The psychotherapist Donald Winnicott claimed that there was no such thing as a baby (Winnicott, 1971) – that a baby only existed in relation to its mother, or primary caregiver. In much the same way, any writing only exists in partnership with the reader, so thank you for choosing to pick up this book, to explore its contents and for us to create something together from the thoughts within these pages and your response to them.

I invite you to take a good look at yourself as you embrace the writing here.

PART ONE

On Reinvention

CHAPTER ONE

The cycle of work life

In this first chapter, I encourage you to open your minds to what we can do to reinvent ourselves, to discover how ideas from psychology can help us to redefine and reshape our future selves. It will show you the importance of embracing the notion that we can reinvent ourselves by changing the way we think, and it will introduce some stories about those who have done just that.

At the beginning it is important to recognize the changeable and unpredictable nature of work. There are ups and downs, emotional roller coasters, learnings and development. The path of our working lives is not always certain; it provides opportunities and challenges. Acknowledging the cyclical nature of working life is vital to our connection to reinvention.

The trajectory of our lives – personal, emotional, professional – rarely runs smooth, and we traverse a bumpy road. There are highs and lows, times when we feel we are storming ahead and times when we fall behind. Working lives are rarely linear, especially in times when the nature of work is changing so dramatically.

We will consider meaning and work, why it is you choose to do what you do, and ask the fundamental question 'Why am I working?'. What are the values that inform your decisions and the motivation behind them?

The changing nature of work

Over the last few hundred years, the nature of work has changed dramatically. We have moved from a predictable, consistent trade or craft, unchanged from one generation to the next, to a working life that is complex, constantly changing and rarely offering us longevity. Developments in technology, big data, artificial intelligence, a global pandemic and shifting cultural attitudes to work have meant that little is certain.

This has led to many of us wondering about our relationship to work: how we identify ourselves, what we want to spend decades of our life focusing on and how we present ourselves to others.

Yet this field of openings offers each of us great opportunities to rethink our purpose, explore our passions and make decisions about how we work and what work we do in ways unthinkable even 50 years ago.

There are also many liminal moments that we experience in our working lives: our first job, a return to work after parental leave, promotion, becoming qualified in our profession, voluntary redundancy or perhaps retirement. We also might experience many life events that are less structural but equally impactful: returning to work after a period of illness, suffering a mental breakdown, working through a relationship split, mourning the loss of someone important, becoming a parent.

We will, throughout our working lives, also have times when change is forced upon us, with mergers, relocations, redundancies and the like. We may have moments of clarity and autonomy when we decide that quitting is what suits us best, or when we choose to experiment with new ways of working, new organizations, clients and roles, choosing to transform ourselves doing what we are able and enthused to do.

When we are at school and all through our younger, developing years, we are asked a question along the lines of 'What do you want to be when you grow up?'. The assumption is that there is one thing for us to identify with, one path to follow and certainty in the evolution of our young selves into that distinctive identity.

I still struggle with the question 'What do you do?' The demand for a quick, neat and understandable answer to a complex question of what we do with our professional and working lives is challenging. The social etiquette of asking 'How are you?', often with little interest in a heartfelt response, might elicit a predictable 'Fine', 'Busy', etc. When asking 'What do you do?', a similarly trite response may be delivered that fails to reveal the depth and breadth of what is going on in our internal and external working lives.

What does the work you do say about your values and the choices you have made about how to live your life?

I'm a teacher.
(But I'm also a poet and a chef.)
I'm a marketing manager.
(But I am also writing a novel, building my self-esteem.)
I'm the lawyer my parents always wanted me to be.
(But I am miserable.)

We exist with multiple selves; our innermost identity perhaps concealed from even those dearest to us, including ourself. The self who perhaps feels doubt and shame and navigates numerous regrets. And the person we present to those we work with, our professional self, our attempts to be authoritative, to conceal our self-doubt and to step into the shoes of our role, the leader, the surgeon, the therapist, the marketing executive.

We also exist as part of a greater whole, representing an organization, a sector or a profession. We may define ourselves as a woman in fintech, or a mental health campaigner, a civil servant or an actor. The way we choose to craft our identity will be explored here, in relation to ourselves (the intrapersonal), to others (the interpersonal) and to the organization or system to which we belong (the systemic).

Ice change

In 2023, the scientific community was excited to discover a new type of ice, amorphous with molecules in a disorganized form, not neatly arranged as with crystalline ice (Rosu-Finsen et al, 2023). This is the main kind of ice found in space with, as yet, unidentified potential uses.

The discovery of this new form with promise but no fixed purpose seems a wonderful metaphor for our subject of reinvention. The notion of freezing and unfreezing is also an emblem of change, made famous by the seminal work of Kurt Lewin (1947).

Lewin was a German-born American psychologist, credited with coining the term 'group dynamics'. He was fascinated by groups, and through his exposure to the horror of the Nazis was committed to researching and creating a fair and benevolent group function.

Lewin developed a formative theory on group change that is helpful to apply to the notion of reinvention. He describes how in order to create permanent change in a group, there needs to be a three-step process: unfreezing, moving and refreezing. Unfreezing is the force needed to break a habit, to overcome inner resistance to change. Once the equilibrium has been disrupted we can move to a new point, a new way of operating. For this to be permanent, Lewin used the metaphor of freezing again, to secure the new way of being.

The coronavirus pandemic presented most of us with a clear example of Lewin's model. What had been solid in terms of patterns of work, social exchange, travel and personal interaction was reformed (unfrozen). What had been certain became uncertain; we would not continue to live our lives as we had, we had to change (move).

As we embraced this change, we moved to the necessary behaviours to stay safe. We stopped touching each other, hid our faces behind masks, washed our hands, stopped commuting, worked from home, and discovered a new normal. This behaviour was encouraged by regular broadcasts, advertising, social consensus (freezing). As lockdown eased and restrictions were lifted, we moved to another phase – more aware of the choices we have in terms of where and how we work, more alert to the fragility of life.

Lewin's model of change can be considered with any change or habit we are trying to break. We may, for example, wish to stop being too apologetic and submissive at work. Our first stage is unfreezing, acknowledging our behaviour, and making a decision to stop our people-pleasing actions. We then move to a different set of behaviours, perhaps avoiding beginning our sentences with 'sorry', or diminishing our contributions; practice that might be enforced with affirmations or journalling. We then need to freeze that change by regular reviews, seeking feedback, or finding a trusted person to check in with.

Any change is made easier with repetition, and acknowledgement that this phase of achievement and what you have conquered is important.

At the end of the chapter you will see an exercise to explore what you might wish to unfreeze, move and refreeze to create the change you want.

Our perspective on the world – encountering an elephant

There is an Indian parable that tells of six blind men encountering an elephant and describing with certainty their experience of the creature. The man standing to its side describes the elephant as a wall, the man at the tail describes the elephant as a piece of rope, the man at the head describes the elephant as a spear and the man alongside the elephant's leg describes the animal as a tree, while the blind man by the flapping ear describes the elephant as a fan.

Each is right in their own way, but in each sticking to their limited views they miss the essence of the truth and the totality of the creature.

This parable was retold as a poem by John Godfrey Saxe in the 19th century, and is an iconic expression of humanity's tendency to claim truth with certainty, despite the limitations of their subjective experience (ignoring other reports of truth that might be different yet equally sound).

We might be described by clients as confident and clear thinking, by our leaders as shy and retiring, by our colleagues as humorous and bubbly and by our siblings as morose and grumpy. Our school friends may see us as studious and bright, and our own assessment might be that we are dim and unaccomplished. All descriptions may hold some truth, but none reflect the totality of our complex selves.

We are like the blind men examining the elephant: we need to zoom out, seek feedback, reflect on ourselves and hold the totality in mind. In order to open up to possibilities and reinvention, we need to step away from a limited view of ourselves, be curious and redefine who we are.

Not working

While this book is primarily focused on work, it might be the case that you're not working at the moment yet still interested in reinvention. You may be unemployed, or between roles, or perhaps you have yet to embark on your working life. Or perhaps the work you do doesn't fit the traditional mould. You may be a creative person pursuing your craft, a volunteer devoting yourself to the greater good, or a carer spending your life caring for another or others.

There may be times during our working lives when our once-prized knowledge and expertise becomes irrelevant. With the rapid development of technology and artificial intelligence, there are many skilled programmers and system developers who are struggling to find a use for their talents.

Research shows us how magnificently resilient we are as human beings, that our capacity for happiness and the ability to rebound from adversity is immense (Hanson, 2018; Haidt, 2006; Kahn, 2019). There are and will continue to be many unpredictable facets of change. This is at the root of reinvention.

Why am I working?

What is it that makes working worthwhile? For each of us there might be a different focus to our sense of purpose, to the foundation of our identity, satisfaction and determination. Having a clear understanding of your relationship to work, how you perceive yourself, what matters to you and what you define as your talents will help you make better future decisions.

The path you choose to follow in life is determined by your values and it is worth thinking carefully about how you wish to live. This might seem so obvious it is not worth saying, yet many of us are carried on the wave of life determined by values that are not our own. Delve deeply and ask yourself what really matters to you.

Meaning and money

The most common way in which our work is valued is through money. Money exchange is in essence a straightforward transactional relationship: services, or goods for money. Yet our relationship with money is complex, and rarely comfortably dealt with head-on. It can often be easiest to enter a state of denial or disengagement, which often causes our financial circumstances to stagnate or even deteriorate. It can be a highly emotional topic, evoking feelings of fear, insecurity and pain.

On the other hand, money can cause us to stay in jobs that no longer satisfy us, encouraging us to take on opportunities for the financial reward rather than the alignment with our values. But we cannot dispute the importance of money: there is a need to pay the bills, feed ourselves and our families, keep warm and live our lives. Money allows us freedom to live in a particular way.

Yet it is a topic often seen as a dirty subject, a taboo to be delicately handled and one that some define as a vulgar topic of conversation, a source of shame. We are more likely to share intimate tales of infidelity or experiences of mourning and loss than we are to detail our fraught relationship with money. The *New York Times* (Wong, 2018) reported that 43 per cent of partners do not know how much their spouse earns.

This extraordinary silence around the topic makes understanding so much harder – we cannot learn about a subject that we do not talk about. This impacts not only our lives, but the organizations and society we function in. Silence around salary can lead to gender inequality and in our relationships to an unfair distribution of social labour (Uwagba, 2021).

Particularly following the economic crash of 2007, there is an aura of distaste around those who pursue financial gain at the expense of other more wholesome values: greedy, covetous bankers for example. Insatiability and acquisition sit uncomfortably on a spectrum that views generosity and passion as worthier. Yet for some money is a core motivator and reason for work. The need for security and recognition may reflect a core need; indeed, money is often an echo of yourself.

The difference between values and goals

We often talk about setting goals to get you to where you want to be. Goals are tangible; there is an end in mind, a certainty about what you want to achieve. There is much sense in this solution-focused approach to reinvention, but before setting goals it is important to be clear about your values:

- Are you committing to action that aligns with the things that matter most to you?
- Are you persuaded to achieve certain goals because of the values of others around you?
- Are you aware of family expectations?
- Are you influenced by sibling choices?
- Are you porous to suggestions on social media about what is important?

You may, for example, become a member of a profession that you know will fill your parents and family with pride: 'My child, the doctor/dentist/teacher/actor/lawyer', etc. Or you may feel pressured to join a family business when your heart is in another industry.

A single identity imposed on you from a young age can limit you. Think about those qualities that are invested in or possibly imposed on you. Do they align with your values and what you consider to be vital in your life?

Do you know what you truly value? What are the non-negotiable facets of your life that inform your choices and guide your plans and actions?

Our values are not static. What is important to us at one stage of life becomes less central at other points. So when our focus is on gaining knowledge and learning, we might value development opportunities over a salary increase. When we are passionate about travel, we may value the prospect of flexible leave over status or a particular title.

Values might also change with age and responsibility: when we become parents or have to care for dependants, hybrid working might be more important than a beautiful working space. What we value at the start of working life may be at odds with our values as we approach retirement.

Values are the things that are important to you. Inevitably things that are important to you change. This does not mean we are flaky or insincere, but that we have the capacity to rethink, to reconsider. Adam Grant, the Wharton professor, implores us to think again (2021); to be more like a scientist constantly exploring hypotheses and then trying something new.

The influential psychologist Edgar Schein builds on the field of values with a longitudinal study and career-history interviews to suggest eight career anchors:

1 technical/functional competence
2 general managerial competence
3 autonomy/independence
4 security/stability
5 entrepreneurial creativity
6 service/dedication to a cause
7 pure challenge
8 lifestyle

Schein argues that these anchors do not change much – our social selves may be different, but once our career anchors are developed, through different experiences, they stay fairly consistent. Although Schein's work is not new – he first published *Career Anchors* in 1993 – the notion of a career anchor is a helpful mindset in exploring values. There is an exercise at the end of the chapter for you to complete to help you clarify what your anchors are in relation to your working self.

Work or career?

A career has connotations of a vocation, a commitment to a set of values and a way of working that carries an individual through stages of development, well-structured and on a path of steady advancement. One might refer to a career in medicine that encompasses key stages of training, early appointments, residency and then qualifications in a specialized area, or a lawyer taking professional exams, getting articles, qualifying, and then going on to establish themselves in a particular area of expert knowledge.

These kinds of career are prescribed: there are certain steps to be taken, formal qualifications to be gained, time spent in particular areas before entry into the professional service and subsequent specialization. This kind of work life is relatively easy to explain and to understand.

However, working life is not always linear and steady, and it is impacted not only by those external markers but also by how the individual feels about their work – how they perceive their work aligns with their values and desire for development. This is likely to fall outside of the traditional hierarchy of formal professions.

Work is an iterative process. We make choices, learn new skills, find ourselves facing fresh obstacles and having to reconnect and learn all over again. It is extremely rare to start work in one organization and stay there until we stop working. We now not only move regularly, but also occupy multiple working identities, perhaps a primary source of income with other work interests alongside.

To work and to love

Freud asserted that the route to a fulfilled life was to work and to love. In most working relationships and workplaces there is a need, however, for boundaries.

We do bring our whole selves to work, with all our experiences, joys, talents and suffering. Yet we do not bring our whole selves to the surface at work – we have a professional identity and social identity, a self that exists in relation to our partner, our children, our different friendship groups. We might embrace our sexual self in intimate relationships, our anxieties with a therapist or coach, but not in the workplace.

This is not to say that you need to hide your vulnerability at work, but rather to be cautious about the places in which you feel psychologically safe and supported. We will examine the role of defence mechanisms and psychological safety later in the book.

Can we really change?

At a recent seminar on transformation, I was asked by an addiction specialist if I thought people can really change. As an author immersed in writing this book on reinvention, my conviction was to say 'Of course'. The 12-step programme developed by Alcoholics Anonymous takes a slightly different view – an admission 'I am an alcoholic', at the start of the process, confirms one's identity as an addict, an enormous first step after potentially years of denial, that defines with brutal honesty one's being. Exploring each of the 12 steps gives hope, strength and guidance for individual recovery, but always begins with that honest admission of personal identity.

The 12 steps focus on addiction, but the practice of self-scrutiny and acceptance sits at its heart. So with this framework one's identity as an addict is always central, but the recovery programme takes you through a process to arrive at forgiveness and growth, a new way of being.

Alongside is the notion that what can be learned can be unlearned, from destructive habits of addiction to learning to say no, from developing new skills to reviewing our priorities at work. So elements of our identity may be fixed, but our capacity to change is not static. This includes the way we view ourselves.

Seeing yourself

In my thirties, I went through a dark period. I failed to see the potential in myself and doubted every part of who I was. I was in a building, walking towards what I thought was the entrance to an office I was due to visit. As I approached, I saw a tall, attractive woman walking with confidence towards me. She didn't move to the side to let me past.

It was only when I hit the glass of the mirror in front of me that I realized I was encountering myself before I had a chance to filter that impression with negative self-talk and derision. It was a moment of revelation for me, and part of my gradual journey to self-acceptance.

A note about the joys of an uncertain future

The world is fractured and there is so much uncertainty: economically, environmentally and psychologically. But the constant, although a cliché, is that change will be persistent, and while we might be reticent to make plans, we do have a choice about how we use our precious time.

There are of course huge differences between us when it comes to privilege and freedom. For some who have savings and a partner or family to support them, their decision to quit a job or retrain is a choice that can be made without financial pressure and risk. For most people, such changes bring with them anxiety and fear about the cost of living and the capacity to pay the bills and to support their dependants. So choice and change is something that needs to be carefully considered.

It can also take time to reinvent, to become qualified in another way of working, or even to just think differently about ourselves. As with any habit change, identity and self-definition can change with repetition, and over time we can break the mould.

Change requires courage; courage that I hope you will find in your own journey of reinvention. The life stories that follow here show that there is much to be lost in pursuing new roles, loss of security, connection, status, finance – but also so much to gain.

There is a Japanese principle that we can call out to that is at the heart of reinvention. Your attitude to change can shift; it is not something that is externally imposed. Yes, we can face extraordinary events that force adjustments to our lives, and we will inevitably experience personal disappointment, but ultimately we have the power to think differently about these changes. The Japanese philosophy of *genchi genbutsu* encourages us to 'go and see for yourself', to observe conditions candidly and make decisions about the obstacles and struggles we face directly.

The exercises that follow at the end of this chapter will allow you to do just that – to go and see for yourself.

REINVENTION STORIES

From award-winning journalist and author to teacher

Lucy Kellaway was awarded an OBE for her services to education in 2021. But her route to teaching and enabling others to join the teaching profession from other sectors was not typical.

A career at the *FT* writing as a journalist and as a satirical columnist might well have been seen as the pinnacle of a stellar career. But in 2017 Kellaway chose to retrain as a teacher. She speaks with passion about her move, describing the stimulation and absence of boredom: 'I'm not remotely repentant about what I've done' (Kellaway, 2017).

Lucy co-founded the charity 'Now Teach' at the start of her transition from journalism to teaching. She went on to make another move within the profession, from maths to business studies, and from South England to the North, continuing her journey of reinvention.

From wrongly convicted criminal to BBC journalist

Raphael Rowe was wrongfully convicted of murder and aggravated burglary in 1990. He served 12 years in prison before being released on grounds of unsafe conviction in 2000, having appealed to the European Court of Human Rights to review the case.

Despite his years incarcerated and the stolen years of his young adult life, Rowe left prison determined to find out who he was and what he wanted to do with his life.

While in prison he studied journalism through a correspondence course and spoke to numerous journalists who by the time his conviction was quashed were editors. He now works as a reporter, television presenter and journalist.

From child prodigy to cognitive scientist and award-winning podcaster

Maya Shankar featured in my previous book *Bounce Back* as an example of ingenuity, loss and renewal. A child prodigy, a violinist mentored by Itzhak Perlman, her identity as a musician ended dramatically following injury. She was a student at Juilliard, with every expectation of a musical career. She is now a cognitive scientist who has worked in the Obama White House and as a Special Advisor to the United Nations.

Since the publication of my last book, she has gone to develop her purpose with the award-winning podcast, *A Slight Change of Plans*, in which she explores the nuances of human behaviour during change.

From productivity plans to plumbing

Nicholas James* gave up a promising career in marketing to become a plumber. He did so at a time of great responsibility, having just become a father and with a huge mortgage.

However, he came to the realization that he just did not want to work in the toxic environment he found himself in, with a boss whose values didn't align with his own. As a new father he was keen to participate in the upbringing of his child, to be able to write and to pursue other interests.

Nicholas is perhaps an unusual plumber: he attended public school, has a law degree and a postgraduate degree in publishing. He now says that retraining to be a plumber was the hardest things he has done.

Two decades into his profession, he has no regrets. He has built a successful business and gets satisfaction from making clients satisfied.

*pseudonym

EXERCISE

Uncovering your values

What values define you? Circle those that mean the most to you, and feel free to add any that are not included in this grid.

Flexibility	Being valued	Integrity	Learning
Recognition	Financial reward	Being challenged	Helping others
Autonomy	Team working	Creativity	Leading others
Innovation	Status	Caring for the Earth	Spirituality
Communication	Risk taking	Loyalty	Professionalism
Security	Curiosity		

These are your values at this point in time, and may change as your life evolves. We may find our priorities and demands lead us to value other areas more intensely than we do now. But it is an important exercise to take stock, to evaluate what matters most to you in your working life.

Reflect on the following questions:

- How do you perceive yourself?
- What did you want to be when you were growing up?
- Does your work environment reflect how you see yourself?
- What is your self-image?
- Analyse your current work self. Does your work allow you to use your talents?
  - Fully
  - Partially
  - Not at all

- Does it align with your values?
  - Fully
  - Partially
  - Not at all
- Does your work meet your material needs?
  - Fully
  - Partially
  - Not at all
- Does your work meet your intellectual/development needs?
  - Fully
  - Partially
  - Not at all
- If the answer to the previous four questions is 'partially' or 'not at all', can you change your work to better meet those needs?
- What adjustments do you need to make to allow your work to align more closely with your needs and values?
- What other role would you consider, and does that role meet the needs and values that matter most to you?

EXERCISE

What is your work lifeline?

Freud is often credited with the observation that the only person with whom you have to compare yourself is your past self. Here we look back as well as to the future as you explore your work lifeline.

Many people focus on the future when thinking about reinvention:

- What will I do now?
- What are my dreams?
- What is my vision for the next six months?
- Where do I want to be this time next year?

All these plans and priorities for the future are useful, but it is also helpful to look back, to consider what has influenced and guided your past decisions. What are the most meaningful events and opportunities that have shaped you?

Take a large blank piece of paper. Consider from the start of your thinking self to the present day:

- What were the highlights of my working life?
- Was I responsible for making these happen?
- Were these external events?
- What were the low points?
- Was I responsible for these?
- Did external circumstances impact events?

Do you notice any repetition?

What have you learned about these moments?

How might these decisions impact your future choices?

EXERCISE

Identifying what you really want, kindly and with self-compassion

Kristen Neff is the queen of self-compassion. Her work encourages us to recognize the ways in which we can be harsh on ourselves and compare ourselves unfavourably with others. When it comes to reinvention, be conscious of your negative self-talk: are you looking at reinvention because you are being too hard on yourself?

Try to use these questions to reframe your desire to change in a more caring and positive way.

Are you using self-criticism to motivate you? For example:

- 'I should have achieved this by now.'
- 'I am so lazy.'
- 'I have been a pushover.'
- 'I am too old/fat/unattractive.'

Can you think of a kinder way of motivating yourself?

- What would your kindest teacher or mentor say?
- Remind yourself of your past achievements.
- Relay the message to yourself that you deserve the chance to develop and be satisfied and stimulated.
- Note the pain and distress of your negative self-judgement.
- Can you reframe your self-criticism in a more compassionate way?
- What would you say to a dear friend to be more supportive and encouraging? For example: 'You are looking forward with enthusiasm,' 'You are giving time to your new project,' or 'You are able to learn from past behaviours that have not been helpful to you'.

CHAPTER TWO

Begin with the endings

You may wonder why endings are so central to the topic of reinvention. Embarking on anything new also means an ending. The assumption that change is good, that it involves things getting better, underpins much of the drive for transformation. Yet this positive perspective on change conceals the pain and vulnerability that is evoked by change and loss. The wisdom that all change is loss, and loss should be mourned, is relevant here (Levinson et al, 1962).

At the start of any reinvention is an ending, a decision to be different, to do something different or to think differently. This can also mean we move from accomplished and at ease to being unsteady, unsure, possibly even incompetent. But for any growth to take place we need to be challenged, and that challenge can be uncomfortable as well as exhilarating.

This chapter is about endings. We will explore the inevitability of loss when we consider reinvention, and examine when one might employ grit to carry on or when we might consider quitting. We will examine regret, transitions and loss of identity, and dig deep into the place of liminal thinking, the in-between place on the boundary of any change.

We need moments of uncertainty, moments of failure, moments of not knowing to push ourselves into new territory. This is often hard, but not as severe as ending before you have even got started. To dismiss opportunities, to fail to pursue ideas, to resist exposure because we are afraid of not achieving, of failing, it is this that leads to a life half lived – and to regret.

Memento mori

Recognizing our mortality is surprisingly difficult. Despite the universal truth that we will all die, the prospect of our own death can be a difficult topic to engage with. The expression 'memento mori', usually translated as 'remember you will die', is a useful motif to retain our sense of the temporal, of the changing nature of all aspects of our life.

We may be in a deep state of angst and pain and cannot see ourselves ever emerging from this despair. 'Memento mori' reminds us that this will pass. The same applies to the highs of life, those moments when everything is glowing and life is full of joy – enjoy it, embrace it, but know such euphoria cannot last. This is not negative talk, but merely an acceptance of the inevitability of endings in our life; that little deaths accompany us at every stage of our life and working life. This was defined by Jacques Lacan as 'petite mort', that after ecstasy there is loss, the moment of realizing that our satisfaction has ended.

The false narrative that we are fed that we should be on a constant high and always feeling good is exacerbated by social media, where inevitably only the good moments are shared. We see the joyful moments, but of course not the less photogenic, chaotic, distressing times accompanying us all. This expectation of a constant flow of positive emotions means we are sometimes ill-equipped to deal with negative emotions (Pink, 2022).

So as we contemplate any reinvention we may focus on what is to come, what our new self might entail, but we should also rest in the place that acknowledges that any fresh experience, identity or endeavour means a loss of sorts.

The pain of regret

Regret can tell us so much about what matters to us. The human ability to feel regret depends on two complex mental abilities: time travel – going back to an event or incident or experience – and storytelling – how we narrate that experience to ourselves and perhaps others; effectively overwriting the present by reconfiguring the past. Regret employs 'if only' thinking, adopting comparative terms that usually sting because so much regret is caught up in self-blame.

Daniel Pink conducted a world regret survey (2023) and found that an overwhelming number of people regretted things that they didn't do, rather than things they had done. Pink found that 'regrets of omission' outnumbered 'regrets of commission' by more than three to one. So failing to attend an important event such as a funeral was deemed a regret more often than taking up a new opportunity.

Some of the specific regrets he identified were:

- missing last opportunities to connect with loved ones
- pursuing higher education
- not travelling when the opportunity was there
- not getting out of a bad marriage/relationship
- behaving with questionable morals when younger, for example bullying kids in school, cheating or shoplifting

Movingly, one of the key early findings from Pink's study was the regret people felt about 'living someone else's life' and not being true to themselves.

It may be impossible to live a full life without at least some regret, but choosing to engage with this book on reinvention is an act that demonstrates your capability to act, to avoid regret in your own working life.

When less is more

A piece of research considering the happiness levels of sports-people winning a medal at the Olympic Games offers us some intriguing data (Gilovich and Medvec, 1995).

Gold medal winners appeared to be the happiest, perhaps understandably so. However, statistical analyses showed that both straight after winning and later at the medal award ceremony, bronze medallists appeared visibly happier than the silver medallists, despite having achieved a lower place on the podium.

Why is this? The bronze medal winner might be thinking: 'At least I won a medal', thinking of the fourth-place winner who won nothing. The silver medallist might, however, be thinking: 'If only I had pushed further, I would be wearing the gold medal'. To imagine success lies only in the narrow bandwidth of the top spot, the gold medal, or the 1 per cent club, limits us.

The notion of counterfactual thinking is relevant to regret. This is where we consider alternative outcomes to what actually occurred, the 'what ifs' and 'if onlys' that relate to past events. It is perhaps key to human thinking to consider what might have been, the alternatives to the choices we actually made. Using counterfactual thinking to review the past can be healthy when used as a way of learning about our past decisions and motivators. For example, we may congratulate ourselves for not taking a path that led others to danger or collapse. However, the healthiest approach is to remember our past decisions, learn from them and focus on the present.

William James identified this 130 years ago in his seminal *Principles of Psychology*:

> So we have the paradox of a man shamed to death because he is only the second pugilist or the second oarsman in the world. That he is able to beat the whole population of the globe minus one is nothing: he has 'pitted' himself to beat that one; and as long as he doesn't do that nothing else counts. (James, 1892)

Comparing ourselves to others leads to regret. When we receive a 5 per cent pay rise we might be rather pleased; finding out our colleague got 10 per cent because they asked for more may make us feel less than pleased.

The question of how we will look back on the lives we lived is often closely associated with regret. A study by a palliative care practitioner (Ware, 2012) explored the regrets that the terminally ill grappled with. These patients, most of whom had only 12 weeks to live, had five standout regrets paraphrased here:

1 I wish I had pursued my dreams, not those expected of me by others.
2 I wish I hadn't worked so hard.
3 I wish I had the courage to express my feelings and speak my mind.
4 I wish I'd maintained my relationships with friends.
5 I wish I'd let myself be happier.

Some psychologists are sceptical of deathbed regrets as there are so many other variables at play: our fragility, the expectations of our loved ones, etc. However, a future focus on our potential regrets in 10 or 20 years' time is recognized as a valuable exercise (Pink, 2022).

Let us consider this asymmetry of regret further. We may express a great deal of regret about taking a particular course of action, for example quitting a job or a relationship, investing in a loss-making deal, choosing to do one thing or another. But we may not regret so explicitly the things we haven't done, staying in the here and now when that is toxic and deflating, for example. Our regrets may be about notable moments and events, yet can also apply to the enduring patterns of behaviour that we do not address, such as tolerating being undervalued or underpaid, or staying in a job that is unsatisfying.

We can flip our thinking about regret and use these intense feelings instead like a springboard to disrupt our cycles of shame and guard against future trauma. George Faller (www.nicabm.com) describes regret as a 'beautiful doorway into deeper views of the self'. We might ask ourselves 'What would have happened if...?' Can we accept our decision making and forgive ourselves?

We may become super-cautious and continue in repetitive patterns of unhelpful behaviour because we fear regretting our choice; in this way regret is an excuse for not doing anything differently, not carrying out appropriate due diligence and walking away to protect our potential hurt.

Regret is something we should embrace and learn from. There is a link between regret and values. So we should engage with it, not ignore it, to listen, to confront and to consider our regrets as a catalyst for meaningful action (Pink, 2022).

Ultimately, regret is a feeling, and it can pass. It can have a protective purpose – we should be curious about our regret and pay attention to that rumination and chattering in our head. What do we need to attend to? What is our regret telling us about what is important to us? What can our regret help us understand about our future choices?

Liminality

When we reinvent ourselves we take with us our experience, our memories, our identity, but we forge new experiences, create new memories and build a new identity. In transition we can be unsettled; we occupy a position on the boundary. We have our past identity fresh in our mind and yet we are not yet at ease in our new place.

The term 'liminality' derives from the Latin word *limen* which translates as 'threshold' (Van Gennep, 1909). The term 'liminal space' was unveiled as a new dictionary.com entry for 2023, as a noun describing a state or place characterized by being transitional or intermediate in some way. The current climate of hybrid working and 'digital nomads' speak to this theme of liminality that, although not new, has a pertinence and relevance in these times of workplace and work style flux.

Van Gennep studied ritual behaviour in individual and collective life, and identified three rites of passage:

1 Separation phase – a time of being disjointed from the rhythm of life.
2 Liminal phase – a time of ambiguity and uncertainty.
3 Incorporation phase – a time of integration and relatively stable new state.

Liminality is a topic explored in anthropology when we consider the sense of being 'up in the air' or 'betwixt and between' whenever we move through life transitions, from birth to death. From baby to toddler, from child to teenager, from teenager to adulthood and adulthood to being an elder and ultimately from life to death. At work these transitions are significant: from trainee to qualified, from apprentice to skilled worker, from follower to leader, from novice to mentor.

Liminality as a process could be seen in the way shown in Figure 2.1.

FIGURE 2.1   The state of liminality

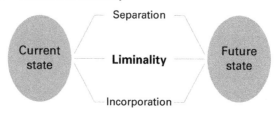

In thinking about liminality in your own working life:

- How are you affected by change at work?
- How do you experience the liminal phase of uncertainty and being 'up in the air'?
- How easy is it for you to adopt a new identity?
- What challenges and tensions exist for you in moving from one state to another?

Each phase marks a fresh start that is preceded by a state of lingering, wondering about the options we have, the possible identities we could occupy. As Ibarra (2004) explains, there are two major challenges we face when trying to change careers: firstly the recognition that 'we are not oneself but many selves', and secondly that it is 'nearly impossible' to consider our reinvention. So in the same way that it is hard to face our mortality, it is also hard to confront a different persona, career or identity.

There are times when we are thrust through a portal: we are made redundant, our organization collapses, or there is a catastrophe that causes us to lose our jobs. Here there is a breakdown that is forced upon us. On other occasions in our working life our current working identity, however unsatisfying or disappointing to us, does offer us containment. There is safety and structure in what we know.

It is not easy to rethink our selves, to have the psychological agility to break through into a new way of thinking.

We will tackle behaviour change in more detail later in the book, but here as we rest on the space between we can consider the challenge of rethinking and reframing, and acknowledge that change happens at the edge. We need to leap to make it happen.

Winnicott's work on the value of the transitional space is hugely valuable here. It marks for Winnicott the space where growth and learning can take place, where he locates play, and indeed all cultural experience. There is no specific time in the lacuna, it is the potential space between the individual and their environment where creativity and transition can exist. We

FIGURE 2.2   The space in between

return to these ideas when we explore planning and uncertainty in the next chapter.

> *The third part of the life of a human being, a part that we cannot ignore, is an intermediate area of experiencing, to which inner reality and external life both contribute. It is an area that is not challenged, because no claim is made on its behalf except that it shall exist as a resting-place for the individual engaged in the perpetual human task of keeping inner and outer reality separate yet interrelated.*
>
> Winnicott, 1971

Transitions

There are so many transitions that we experience in life: socially, intellectually, spiritually, politically and culturally. The changes we experience at work can impact our identity, our comfort in our body, our sense of who we are.

It can be difficult to navigate our working lives when undergoing significant transitions. They can transform our perceptions of ourselves, and will inevitably have an impact on our working lives when we spend so many hours of the week at work.

In some cases, it can also lead to alienation or ostracization within your work community. Take, for example, the transition of a transgender person. Rather than engaging, listening and being compassionate, others may not understand, may air their personal opinions or otherwise make things more difficult. For an individual who is already undergoing the intense experience of a gender transition, their work life can become a barrier to achieving the respect and compassion they deserve.

Stepping into a new way of being, particularly when surrounded by people who are different to us, can lead to misunderstanding and a sense of alienation. In many working cultures, it may be easiest to fit in and hide in the crowd – and anyone who doesn't becomes an outsider who feels uncomfortable or ostracized. Working culture can develop around people who are 'like us', so when we encounter people from smaller communities they may feel not known and not engaged with.

Knowing when to go

Perseverance and commitment are admired qualities. Staying the course, working through difficulties, finishing what we started; these are all attributes that are exalted. The language around the topic is very assured and upbeat – 'determination', 'powering through', even being 'heroic'.

However, there are times when the course of action that serves us best is not continuing along a difficult path, but choosing another path altogether. Recognizing that despite our best efforts in a profession, working with a start-up or alongside someone toxic, it is time to leave. The language around leaving is much less positive: tropes of 'letting go', 'abandoning hope' even 'cowardice'.

Here we will explore and consider when it is time to step back, to acknowledge the difference between possibility and ending.

Passion and perseverance has been highlighted and popularized through the work of Angela Duckworth and her book *Grit* (2016). She explores ideas of mastery, of persevering with difficult things until you become excellent, and the difference between talent and determination. Never suggesting we are all equally talented, she does, however, debunk the idea of expertise lying in the hands of the few masters, the prodigies, and opens up excellence and success to all those prepared to do the hard work with purpose and guts over time.

Her work has opened the conversation about steady, focused work with excitement and enthusiasm. *Grit* encourages us to reframe challenges with our mindset, a topic we will explore in more detail later in the book. There is a great deal to admire in this approach of deliberate practice, focus and commitment to action.

The idea that excellence can be achieved through effort, hard work and single-mindedness is very much in the spirit of this book. Attending to your future focus, deciding what works for you and what no longer works for you is part of that process.

However, there are times when we need to decide: is this a time for grit, or is this a time to quit?

We might be working with toxicity, in an industry that does not align with our values, or for people we no longer respect or trust. We may be at the point of deciding that we want to retire from a particular role, to take the opportunity that voluntary redundancy is offering us. Our home life may have changed, and we might want to rethink our priorities. A momentous event in our lives might have caused us to rethink, to ask the key question: 'Why am I doing this?'

Learning how to quit is a skill. To take control of your destiny, to have 'agency', the term social scientists adopt to describe the degree to which people believe that they have the power to shape their world. There is of course luxury and privilege in such work choices. When you are desperate for work in order to survive, the idea of quitting might seem abhorrent. We are also programmed for cognitive bias that makes change difficult; the preference for the status quo that steers us away from the path of change.

The subject of 'revelatory autonomy', the moral right to discover ourselves and who we can become after making transformative choices, was described in a study conducted at Cambridge on self-authorship. It describes the idea that we will never know our future desires, values and preferences without the capacity to make those transformative choices.

The ability to see that the person we've become is the product of decisions that we made for ourselves is very important.

Akhlaghi, 2022

Such decisions might mean taking a pay cut to pursue a career change. There may be many interested parties who might be impacted by that choice, and who therefore try to influence the person making the decision. Such influences might relate to concerns about status, or a rejection of lifestyle choices by peers or family members who benefitted from the lifestyle. The Cambridge study highlights the individual's right to make voluntary choices that create transformative experiences.

Akhlaghi's study focuses on autonomy, but context is also important; thinking carefully about the conditions in which we should decide to leave work, to quit a project, or to end a partnership might involve creating a good decision-making environment. That environment might welcome another trusted person who is not immersed and invested in the situation, to seek their perspective and allow space to think.

Annie Duke is a cognitive scientist turned poker player, turned academic, turned author, turned consultant and speaker. She speaks and writes eloquently about the thread that runs through all her life occupations – learning under uncertainty. She has written a book extolling the unsung benefits of leaving and endings: *Quit: The power of knowing when to walk away* (2022).

In examining the science of quitting, Duke says poker is a game that thrives on quitting. She thinks we should quit a lot more. Her writing reveals her own story grappling with quitting, as well as giving guidance on how to make decisions that may lead you to quit. We might imagine people's negative response to our decision to leave, yet much of this negative chatter might live solely in our heads.

When deciding whether to leave, we should remember:

- Situations and context can change – we don't need to stick with a bad choice.
- Our own preferences, lifestyle or circumstances can change.
- We can always get some help.
- You can draw boundaries to decide when you will quit (a time, a target, etc).
- Goals can be set with an 'unless' clause.
- Decisions are not absolute – you can return and change course, or get back to ideas previously rejected. You can adopt a more exploratory mindset; you can be creative and courageous.

The matryoshka principle

The metaphor of the matryoshka, the Russian doll with multiple dolls resting inside the outer shell, is helpful in thinking about our multiple work identities. The fact that we cannot see the smaller dolls inside does not mean that they are not there. The object within the object also recognizes the multiple identities we can hold, over time and in different circumstances.

One of the challenges of reinvention is leaving behind the person who we once were. In leaving a profession, or a relationship or a business, much of our comfortable self-identity is abandoned. The contradiction exists that in working life we strive for comfort, yet only progress when we encounter discomfort. Mastery of a particular skill, area of knowledge or way of being can bring pleasure and pride, but to reinvent we need to move away from the cushion of comfort.

If our social crutch is the way we introduce ourselves as an entrepreneur, or working mother, or activist, or engineer, and we decide that these roles no longer suit our values, our circumstances or our purpose, we can feel derailed and distinctly uncomfortable.

The changing work identities we experience in our 20s, 30s, 40s, 50s, 60s and beyond are points of liminal struggle, but also opportunities to emerge fresh, to become another. The roles, functions and skills we occupied previously remain with us as building blocks and part of the rich hinterland of our working identity. We do not need to discard those identities entirely, merely to recognize their place in our past as we move forward to reinvent ourselves.

This also highlights the complexity of quitting and reinvention. To hold in mind the nesting set of our identity that relates not only to our functional selves, but also to our body, mind, soul and spirit.

Endings are hard

In embracing endings and loss, it is worth remembering that it is tough to lose your job; it is hard to be rejected; it is challenging to find your colleague is promoted and you are not; it is taxing to be made redundant. We may embrace the inevitability of endings, but also know that loss in all its forms can be difficult to engage with.

Endings are difficult, and yet they are part of every beginning. We may gain a new perspective, a new role, new opportunities or a new identity, but leave behind the sense of who we were. That longing for the past might romanticize what has been.

Death and grief are lifetime companions, yet facing our mortality, despite its certainty, can take a great deal of thought and work; some may say a lifetime's work. Endings at work might not have the same gravity as personal loss, yet they are made of the same emotional ingredients. All loss reminds us of other loss. We lose someone, we lose our identity, our role, our status, and that then creates a new normal that must be embraced.

For reinvention to take place, it is that place of new normal we must strive to occupy.

REINVENTION STORIES

From accomplished sportsman to female model and activist

Munroe Bergdorf is a model, writer, guest editor of *Vogue* and activist. She transitioned from he to she, going through many painful and angst-ridden times before emerging as a fulfilled and contented woman living her best life.

As a teenager she was a swimming sensation, ranked 11th in the country, a top high jumper and a talented middle-distance runner. Yet she took no pleasure in her sporting prowess.

Her book, the story of her transformation, *Transitional*, was released in February 2023. Her capacity to write a manifesto for the marginalized alongside her life story has been widely applauded, and she champions truth, a far cry from the bullied, sexually abused, traumatized and confused young person she was. She sits on the editorial board for L'Oréal, guiding the beauty company on matters of equality, diversity and inclusion.

Munroe champions her community from a platform that allows conversations about the challenges of being trans, queer and misunderstood.

What's in a name?

When Hillary Rodham married Bill Clinton, she saw no reason to change her name – neither she nor he saw it as important. However, the citizens of Arkansas where Bill was Governor felt differently.

Hillary was not a typical first lady. From the 1970s onwards people were constantly asking her to change: not just her name, but the way she spoke, the way she dressed, the way she interacted with the public. Change was forced on her in terms of her identity, her role and how she presented herself to the world – she did not fit the mould. Her name was central to her professional identity. She had taught, published and practised as a lawyer with her name.

When the Clintons became parents, the name issue was significant for the voting public, with many citing her 'different' name as central to Bill's loss of position as Governor. Hillary decided to be known as Hillary Rodham Clinton – something that through a historical lens feels outdated but, at the time, taking a balanced assessment, was the right decision for them.

Her name allowed others to accept her as the Governor's wife. So the compromise, this loss of identity, gave Hillary scope to continue her work.

Business to academia, on the outside pushing in

Mark Stringer spent 30 years in a business career before becoming an academic, lecturer, Programme Director and Head of Department at a prestigious London university.

Entering the world of academia later in his career, at the age of 54, opened up the potential for freedom, creativity and intellectual pursuit, but also brought enormous challenges with the messy, precarious state of contemporary higher education careers. The move into a role with fewer prospects and a less-than-certain path to senior status, in a field that can be cruelly competitive and slow to change, was bold and courageous.

Mark, also a musician and a creator of soundscapes, reflects on a growing sense that, by coming to academia late and in a non-traditional manner, he is not only moving 'up the hill backwards', akin to the David Bowie song, but doing so with weights on his ankles. How to respond to unconscious desire and the individual liminal state that this has created?

He describes himself as on the outside, happily pushing in.

From half dead to living fully

Michael Rosen, the acclaimed children's poet laureate, has had several close encounters with death. He has published prolifically and shared his experience of endings with his readers and in his broadcasting career. He spent a year at medical school before studying English at Oxford and has a lifelong love of poetry. He worked at the BBC, as an employee, as a freelancer and as a broadcaster.

Why then does he feature in a story of reinvention? Michael wrote about the death of his beloved son in *Michael Rosen's Sad Book*, but had his own close encounter with death in 2020. Michael's life was saved by the NHS during the Covid-19 pandemic. He spent 48 days in intensive care.

He had to learn to live again, and wrote *Many Different Kinds of Love: A story of life, death and the NHS* about his experience of being hospitalized and his recovery. His poem 'These are the Hands' was written in celebration of the 60th anniversary of the NHS, but became emblematic during the pandemic.

After his recovery Michael continues to work prolifically, adapting his school visits to a virtual environment, but he says 'I am not who I was'.

Endings and new beginnings: the seven-year itch

Arielle Steele (née Tchiprout) worked for seven years at a major publishing house. From her early days as an intern to her role as senior editor, she has interviewed and worked with legends like Dolly Parton, Jane Fonda and Brené Brown. As Health and Wellbeing Editor for three of the UK's biggest selling monthly magazines, she made the leap to working freelance in 2023 with the spirit of Taylor Swift accompanying her, in that 'nothing safe is worth the drive'.

Her decision to quit and go freelance came at a point in her career where she felt 'deep down, that I needed something different'. She was comfortable and secure in her job with the satisfaction that she knew she was good at it.

But a rocky year of grief reminded her that life is fleeting, and that you have to take risks and make changes when those feelings come up. She mulled it over for a few months; thought about all the things she could achieve if she left her role, ran the numbers for how much money she'd need to make to match her salary. Probably with an idealized vision of what freelancing looked like, she gave herself a deadline, held her breath and took the plunge.

The first day, she felt as if she was skiving from work, and was suddenly hit with the realization that she'd left the job that had become her home and identity for seven years. Quickly she found her creativity flooding back; with the space to find what made her tick, and with a renewed passion and zest for life.

Still early in her freelance journey, Arielle says: 'It's certainly been full of ups and downs so far. But the highs are worth the lows because my life seems so much more open now and fizzing with opportunity.'

Teenage model who became editor of *British Vogue*

Edward Enninful OBE was born in Ghana to a military father and seamstress mother. He emigrated to London at the age of 13. Spotted on the tube, he became a model at 16 but soon became involved in fashion styling, becoming one of the youngest ever fashion directors at 18. Enninful's health has been challenging: he is partially blind, with less than 50 per cent hearing, and has a blood disorder: sickle cell and thalassaemia. Experiencing racism and homophobia, he has championed inclusivity, diversity and disability throughout his career and notably as the editor of *British Vogue*. His attitude to life is distinctly forward-focused, always moving and developing. He shared his life story in his 2022 autobiography, *A Visible Man*.

EXERCISE

Carpe diem

The Roman poet Horace might have been surprised that his sanguine guidance to 'seize the day' was still so relevant 2,000 years later. We are confronted with many opportunities at work; some may be experiences we are longing to engage in, but feel that we are too busy or not yet qualified to embrace.

This exercise encourages you to avoid procrastination, to say yes, to sign up, to make the call, to start the project or connect with the person who reached out to you.

Spend 10 minutes making a list of the current opportunities in your life, no matter what the magnitude or apparent relevance.

What action can you take to grab these opportunities?

Plan and schedule, do it now.

You may be thinking of sharing your thoughts among your network, nominating yourself for a project role, walking at lunchtime rather than eating at your desk, taking a course, stopping apologizing for your contributions, walking tall and improving your posture, taking a breath before you engage with a difficult colleague, asking for a pay rise – the opportunities are endless.

EXERCISE

Can I fix this?

There are some occasions when we make a simple mistake that can be rectified. In these circumstances, consider if you can rescue the situation. What could you do to resolve this mishap or regrettable action? This fix may or may not work, but could help you to bring closure and help you to stop ruminating.

Identify what it is that you regret and that you can do something about. (Perhaps you failed to acknowledge a colleague's contribution and took credit yourself, or you failed to speak out about bad practice and stayed silent, or you failed to acknowledge a bereavement or illness because you felt uncomfortable.)

What can you do? (Acknowledge the contribution made by your colleague at the next public event, apologize for not speaking out against bad practice and make a public commitment to do so in future, acknowledge the suffering/loss even if it was not an immediate action.)

Schedule tasks for anything you identified above, and do them.

EXERCISE

Should I stay, or should I go?

This is a simple exercise exploring change. It can be difficult to take a leap and move from perhaps a steady and secure role into the unknown. All change is challenging in some ways: as we discussed in Chapter 1, all change is loss and needs to be mourned. But it is also helpful to fully explore your desires and the disadvantages of the here and now and the future.

Carefully consider the prompts below and list as many reasons you can for each. This will build your understanding of what staying and quitting mean to you:

- Great reasons why I should stay...
- Great reasons why I should quit...
- The downsides of staying...
- The downsides of quitting...

EXERCISE

Mental time travel

Mental time travel, also referred to as Episodic Future Thinking (EFT), allows you to envision potential futures. It gives your brain a chance to consider new possibilities and offer clues as to what is yet to come. If you are struggling with reinvention, with the prospect of leaving your current working identity and adopting a new identity, this exercise allows you to prepare neural pathways that will consider possibilities.

This exercise can also be adapted to allow you to explore regret and learn lessons: will you be happy with your future imagined self?

Try this simple 30-second exercise: Imagine yourself starting your working day tomorrow. Think of the way your day will start: where will you be, what will you be wearing, who will be with you, what tasks will you tackle? What challenges will you face? What are you looking forward to? What are you dreading?

Now try this more challenging 30-second exercise: Imagine yourself starting your working day a year from today. Think of the way your day will start: where will you be, what will you be wearing, who will be with you, what tasks will you tackle? What challenges will you face? What are you looking forward to? What are you dreading?

Now try this even more challenging 30-second exercise: Imagine yourself starting your working day 10 years from today. Think of the way your day will start: where will you be, what will you be wearing, who will be with you, what tasks will you tackle? What challenges will you face? What are you looking forward to? What are you dreading?

CHAPTER THREE

Planning your future self

Creating plans can be a vital part of ensuring success. Break down the things that need to be done in order to achieve your desired behaviour change, goal or transformation. This is the foundation of much work in the behavioural sciences, and indeed is seen as the behavioural insight most important to create behavioural change by psychologists such as Angela Duckworth, author of *Grit* (2016), renowned for her work on passion and perseverance.

But the plan alone will accomplish nothing. We need to be clear about what we want to achieve. We need to know how we are going to accomplish the elements of the plan. We need to know when this will happen and where the action will take place. Planning requires work.

Before we create the plan there is a great deal to be done, exploring what it is you want to achieve, testing and playing with different ideas before you reach some clarity about what your priority is for the shorter and longer term.

Plans don't change minds.

Milkman, 2022

We need to have clarity and focus; this is essential before any successful plan is made. I could create a very thorough and practical plan to swim the Channel. It might have a clear training schedule, timescales, an identified support team and even details of the most effective and protective barrier cream. But such a plan would be useless. I have no desire and no intention to ever swim across the Channel.

A large part of the battle of creating a successful plan is knowing what it is we want to achieve. We need to confront uncertainty and devote time and energy to contemplating what it is we want to achieve.

Here we will explore ideas and tools to help you delve into your desired reinvention and the plan that will best help you to get there.

Planning matters when we consider reinvention. Doing nothing in the hope that wonderful and dramatic things will happen is hopeful, but ultimately unhelpful. The thought needs to be translated into some plans and some action. This chapter highlights the value of applying psychologically informed approaches to planning, and thereby to better understand some of the deeper complexities and dynamics of this part of reinvention.

The desired destination?

When we imagine alternative ways of being, we often leap to the final stage, to visions of running our new business, to being appointed to a role, to arriving at our desired destination. We may have a yearning for a different version of ourselves, yet the route to that desired outcome is not always so clear. We can't manifest our futures, but knowing the destination is the first step to preparing a practical plan.

This chapter examines the possible, the probable and our desirable futures. It also faces uncertainty head on and looks at the tools, techniques and plans that can take you to your desired future self.

Making the leap

We learn by doing, and each new experience is part answer and part question.

Ibarra, 2004

The way we plan, and enact our plans, changes when we move from space to space as marked in Figure 3.1.

At ease: here we are comfortable and unlikely to plan to change. We are settled and know what to expect. Perhaps we are also glad that we are not being pushed outside of the zone of our capability. It is safe and sound; in this space one might feel inclined to stay put.

However, this zone is not one we always rest in readily. It could be the place where we feel anxious about rocking the boat, fearful of change and therefore unwilling to stretch our boundaries and test our abilities by stepping into the unknown. Such 'stuckness' could relate to previous attempts to shift that have been unsuccessful, therefore we are frightened to try again, or we could be lethargic and lacking in self-belief. Some may also feel 'I have been doing this for so long,' or 'Could I do anything else?' or 'Am I capable of change?'.

A comfortable place: this position relates to a relaxed and easy place of learning. This may be relevant to those times when

FIGURE 3.1   The comfort zone

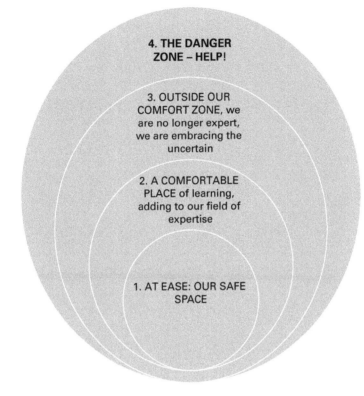

4. THE DANGER ZONE – HELP!

3. OUTSIDE OUR COMFORT ZONE, we are no longer expert, we are embracing the uncertain

2. A COMFORTABLE PLACE of learning, adding to our field of expertise

1. AT EASE: OUR SAFE SPACE

our progress is structured within a scheme of learning, when there are steady steps to take to develop our understanding or to progress to the next stage of competence. This might relate to a training contract, an apprenticeship, or a newly qualified role when we are still being developed and probably monitored. Our progression is assured within a system that guarantees we are capable of the next steps that we need to take.

Outside our comfort zone: here we are no longer at ease and need courage to make the leap. It could mean a complete change of career path or embracing a whole new set of skills. Examples might include those who have worked for long periods in a particular sector, those moving from education to business, or from one profession to an alternative sphere, perhaps from law to a creative industry. This space also refers to those who retrain, who begin to see the world differently through the lens of their newfound knowledge.

This stage perhaps relates best to the part of the conscious competency cycle: we know we are not yet accomplished in this field, yet we are going to attempt to make it work and to learn along the way.

The danger zone: here we do need help. Perhaps we are responsible for the security or safety of staff or clients, and our lack of knowledge or expertise could cause harm. This can be a fertile learning space, but needs to be approached with caution. There is no harm in speaking up, saying: 'I do not know what to do here, I need guidance and training to ensure no damage is caused'.

Rushing through policy, signing legal documents without proper counsel, investing clients' money without adequate understanding of the markets: these plus many more potentially harmful actions demonstrate that we need to learn more before we act. It does not mean that we cannot ultimately take on these demanding tasks, but that we need to recognize our skill and knowledge gaps and fill them before we leap.

The conscious competency cycle is a useful learning model when considering new skills or when transforming our behaviour. Exploring the psychological state we occupy when facing a reinvention can help us discover our blind spots and open our eyes to areas where we need to develop. The state of unconscious competence, being in a position of expertise and quiet confidence, may be our goal, but using this model we can mindfully work through the different states necessary to reach this point of flow.

The model suggests a steady progression through the four states of learning, but as with any experience of learning it is an active process that can be iterative as we broaden and develop our understanding. Welcoming feedback, reflecting on our experience and

FIGURE 3.2   The competency cycle

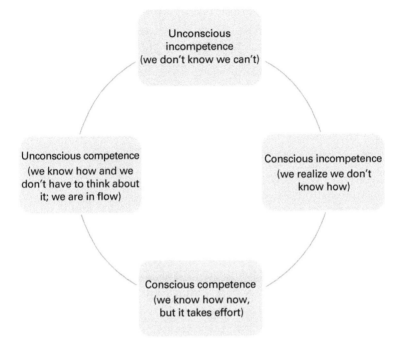

checking back to review our progress are activities that can aid our progression through this cycle.

The competency cycle is helpful for individual learning, but is also useful when working with others. There are downsides to being in a continuous state of unconscious competency – we might imagine others are equally at ease with a task or activity, and not recognize the effort required from them to deliver.

Take the example of deep listening. We may be blissfully unaware that others perceive us as poor listeners, more interested in what we have to say than listening to the other. This would place us in the position of unconscious incompetence. We may receive some feedback or even note unsuccessful communication patterns, so realize we need to try to show interest in our interlocuter, to not interrupt: here we are in the stage of conscious incompetence.

We then begin to practise, to listen without the need to pounce with our contribution, to tolerate the pause. We might note our progress: here we are in a phase of conscious competence. Finally, our new way of listening becomes part of the way we communicate with others. We do not need to remind ourselves to listen, we can do so naturally and with curiosity. Deep listening has become part of the way we communicate; we have become unconsciously competent at this valuable communication skill.

Career construction theory

Savickas' (2020) career construction theory (CCT) can help us delve into the way we plan our next stage meaningfully. His work on the self-constructing process involved in career building and making sense of our vocational pathways calls not only on our self-awareness and self-understanding, but also an acknowledgement of the systems in which we operate. So this might relate to the culture and values of the organization you are in, but also the global events that occur as you build your vocational life.

The work we carried out centuries ago, often on the land and similar from one generation to the next, involved survival and little else. We worked physically rather than intellectually, to keep a roof over our heads and to feed the family and perhaps livestock. This way of working bears little resemblance to our current needs for self-actualization, development and meaning in our working lives.

We also have agency in the way in which we choose to work. Where and how we work can matter deeply: do you plan and hope to prioritize an ability to work remotely, for example? Or do you value an in-person working environment that is for you an important factor in making work better?

Savickas offers a way to break down the self-construction process, with the overarching recognition that such self-construction exists within the context of the systems and societies in which we operate – so in a sense it is a co-constructed meaning. He refers to career construction theory as an interpretive and interpersonal process whereby we shape our identity and build a career. It is a way of tackling our working lives in a conscientious, deliberate, organized and decisive way.

The following elements of CCT function together to reveal the way in which we create meaning about our vocational choices.

Self-organizing:

- What are the knowledge, competencies, beliefs and experiences that can help me build self-awareness and evaluate my working self?
- What meaning have I attached to the choices that I have made?
- What do I want the work I am doing to say about me in the world?
- Have I stopped to evaluate my working identity?

Self-regulating:

- How do I control the self (by the self); where is my self-direction, self-management, goal-setting?
- How do I mark and assess my progress?
- What am I doing to preserve self-esteem?
- What can I become by doing work?
- How do I want to be seen?

Self-concerning:

- What symbolic representations do I adopt to make sense of myself, in my social roles and in the world?
- What do my thoughts mean?
- What career stories do I tell myself and the world?
- How do I present myself?
- What does this mean to me?

Allowing yourself time to consider your work in the context of these meaning making tools is not a given. We make huge decisions quickly, and do not always reflect as deeply as we could about our motivations and desires.

Self-doubt

A big part of our resistance to creating change or even considering reinvention is the influence of self-doubt – the nagging inner narrative that says we cannot change, we do not have the skills, talents or potential. We may wonder:

- Could I ever do that?
- Am I capable?
- Am I clever enough?
- Am I too old?
- Do people like me ever do things like this?
- Could someone who sounds like me do this?
- Do I look right?

Essentially, we are asking questions about belonging. We may hold in mind an imagined sense of the kind of person that occupies the role we are longing for; we may question our gender, our ethnicity, our age. Could someone like us ever achieve this?

However, internal misgivings can be turned into an asset. Kevin Cokley (2018) has studied the psychology of self-doubt, and explores ideas of feeling fraudulent and not as smart as accolades and compliments suggest. He proposes that such doubt can lead to an urge to prove our worthiness, resulting in a work ethic that creates results. Those who doubt themselves work harder to address their sense of inadequacy.

He also urges those who suffer from self-doubt to remember their accomplishments through the practice of keeping a work diary that documents their successes – as it is easy to forget the things that have gone well. Self-doubt in this way can actually drive us to success: because we are not lazy or presumptuous about our talent and ability, we work hard to contribute, to be successful.

Being intentional about noting our successes can help us reimagine ourselves. We talk more about the notion of imposter syndrome in Chapter 7.

Procrastination

The counter stance to overpreparation and hard work is procrastination. There are times when we know action is needed, and yet we find time to do everything and anything but the thing that is a priority. These are the occasions when we avoid the more challenging things on our to-do list, and instead organize our books or our spice racks. We send unimportant emails instead of addressing the difficult decisions we have to make. We go online shopping or scroll on our phones.

This is not about laziness. More likely we are afraid of the consequences of dealing with the task, of making the wrong decision, about being ill-equipped to address the challenge we are putting off. It is ironic that we put off deciding, assuming that no decision is made, yet postponing a decision in itself is decisive.

Much of the fear we associate with poor decision making is linked to our relationship with failure. We fear that we will make a mistake, that we will be seen to be stupid or reckless or uninformed. Yet, as we are culturally beginning to recognize, failure is inevitable for growth, for life! It is only by trying, failing and learning that we can live a full life. This was explored in depth in my previous book, *Bounce Back* (Kahn, 2019).

Wharton Professor Katy Milkman offers some useful guidance for those who display what she refers to as 'present bias', to steer those who procrastinate about long-term goals. She writes about creating restraints that anticipate temptation, essentially reducing freedom in service of a greater goal (Milkman, 2022). So when we are procrastinating about action that will benefit our longer-term work aspirations, our reinvention, we could consider one of these commitment devices:

- A public pledge to get something done.
- A limitation on freedom until something is achieved.
- A small, frequent commitment is more effective than a large, infrequent one.

In praise of lists

One tool to help with such commitment devices is making lists.

I am a lover of lists – on my phone, handwritten in notebooks, typed, and printed as hard copies for me to scribble on and revisit. Some will agree that crafting a list is a soothing process. It is a way of capturing everything that is preoccupying our minds, the things that must be done today, the things that ideally will be tackled in the future. This is planning in its simplest form – noting the things that need to be done.

Yet not all lists are created equal.

List 1:

- butter
- coffee
- houmous
- tomatoes
- garlic
- olive oil

List 2:

- new job
- move house
- find a life partner
- get a master's degree

- run a marathon
- write my will

The reason the first list is likely to be accomplished is that it is simple to understand, within reach of most, not overly resource hungry, accessible, affordable and short.

List two is a lifetime's work. One could more productively break down the elements of this life list to allow you some hope of making progress.

So, to get a master's degree:

- research institutions
- read two articles a week to ensure I am making the right subject choice
- take time to explore with a thinking partner 'Why do I want to do this?'
- make financial arrangements
- share my plans with those it will impact: work, family, dependents
- explore funding
- talk to graduates of the programme
- examine timings
- fix a timescale

You could further break down each element of this secondary list:
- research institutions:
  - look at league tables
  - attend at least three open evenings
  - look at online evaluations of the programme
  - compare and contrast term times and flexibility
  - evaluate value for money
  - consider teaching quality
  - find out tutor/student face-to-face time
  - explore the library
  - ask to speak to the programme director

Often we limit our chances of success by setting huge, demanding goals that are unrealistic. We need to look to the future, but take a view on the small steps we need to get us there. The lists we write can then be revised and refreshed, but with satisfaction rather than frustration.

When plans go wrong

Rather than acknowledge that the path we have taken is not actually what we wanted, often we carry on, pursuing the dream, digging deeper into the original goal. We must, we tell ourselves, stay on track; our determination to succeed does not tolerate a diversion or indeed another road altogether. We might find ourselves in the job that we imagined we would love; our party conversation is ready: 'I am a doctor'; 'I am a chef'; 'I am the MD of my own company'. Yet these dreams fulfilled might not be satisfying you and giving you the life you had imagined.

What does it take to acknowledge that this is not all you hoped for? That the passion and perseverance you have invested has not actually materialized in the way you had hoped?

There are many celebrated mountaineers, climbers who have reached the summit in record time, who are seen as heroes. This is the ironic reality even when they do not make it home from their trip. Success is seen to be about getting to the top; it is not about the more important achievement of returning safely down the mountain.

Other examples abound in sport – sportsmen and women who refused to quit, and ruined their bodies and their mental health as a result. We think of Muhammad Ali who refused to walk away when his life and health would have been vastly improved by an earlier retirement, rather than the stubborn perseverance and life-limiting illness he experienced.

Simone Biles, the exceptional Olympian and gymnast, pulled back from participation in the 2020 Tokyo Olympics because of stress. As she describes it, 'Walking away from the Olympic Games was a win in itself'. She could have suffered and pressed on. Instead, she put herself first and became a winner and a role model in another way. When she eventually returned for the US Championship in 2023, she made history by becoming the first gymnast to win the tournament eight times. As Adam Grant (2021) states in *Think Again*:

> For the record, I think it is better to lose the past two years of progress than to waste the next twenty.

So, when planning our future selves we need to think about our hopes in context. To think carefully about what we are hoping to achieve in the round. Does the goal we have in mind get us to the top of the proverbial mountain, but mean we are so burned out we cannot get back down again? Do we sacrifice our health and relationships to get to the imagined place of victory?

If our ambitions are financial, what are we hoping to satisfy when we reach that milestone? When we are a millionaire, or a billionaire, will we have arrived? Or will that goal simply be replaced by a desire for greater financial success?

Pause and the space of silence

Human beings are not designed to run without a break, without a chance to refresh. The importance of the pause, the chance to reset and regenerate, is vital to our development (Poynton, 2019). Sometimes we are moving so fast to reach our summit that we do not stop and reflect about whether that is what we truly want, or indeed if we have the capacity to think beyond that achievement. A pause in our conversation or our thinking and internal chatter can also give us the space to consider and reflect on our plans.

In my work as an academic and lecturer training and coaching psychologists, I encourage students to engage in the shift from theory to practice, where ideas and models are explained and then tried out. There is often a big difference between intellectually understanding an idea and expediently applying that idea in your practice.

One of the most valuable lessons of a helping professional is the place of silence. This in itself is not a lacuna of inactivity, but space where new thoughts and reflections can emerge. When we rush to fill a gap, to keep the polite rhythm of conversation going, we take away this space for careful contemplation. In the demand for a successful-looking exchange, our interlocuter is denied the pleasure and the depth of deep thinking.

We can turn this inwards too: the constant chatter and inner demands alongside the external demands to contribute and to be 'on' can mean that we have little time to rest in silence, to allow thoughts to emerge freely without a demand for an answer or a solution. Allowing ourselves time to walk in silence, without our headphones, without a companion, is refreshing in every sense of the word.

A thirst for constant stimulation, entertainment and knowledge can be enriching, but creating some space to think, to process all the experiences, ideas and possibilities, allows an opening place for true reinvention.

One of the world's greatest historians and philosophers, Yuval Noah Harari, takes regular time to embrace silent retreats, to quiet his mind and allow new thoughts to emerge. He refers to how much he learned about himself on his first meditation retreat in *Sapiens* (2014). The instruction to 'do nothing' is far more demanding than it sounds. Our minds are constantly working to avoid facing difficult and painful realities. Sitting in silence can offer us an insight into the patterns of our own minds.

So allowing yourself time to think, to give yourself what Nancy Kline refers to as sanctuaries for the human mind (1999), can give us the thinking time, in silence and solitude, that can reveal and unlock our ideas allowing us to plan ahead.

Identity foreclosure

This is a notion we touched on at the beginning of this book, when we explored the tired old question 'What do you want to be when you grow up?'. Prematurely attaching your working identity to a profession leads to a fixed mindset, closing off opportunities that might better suit your growing self.

Identity foreclosure, or premature commitment to a particular work identity without due diligence, was introduced by the psychologist Erik Erikson and built upon by James Marcia in

FIGURE 3.3   Development of identity model

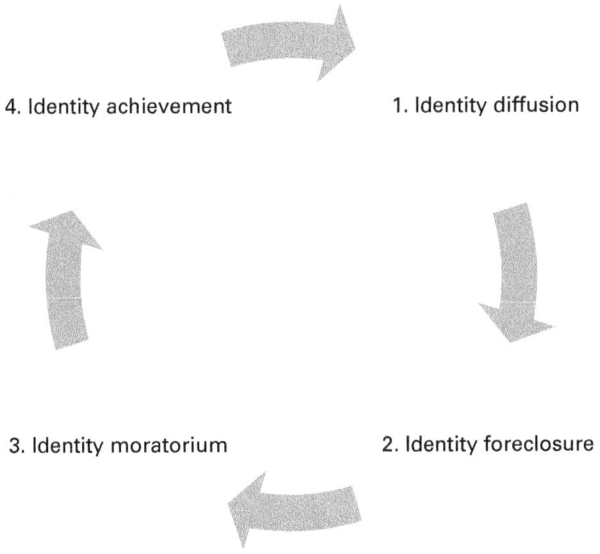

4. Identity achievement 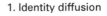   1. Identity diffusion

3. Identity moratorium   2. Identity foreclosure

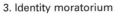

Cieciuch and Topolewska (2017); Erikson-Marcia tradition

63

the 1960s. Their work has been influential in the field of developmental psychology.

The stages of identity development (see Figure 3.3) are as follows:

- Identity diffusion: Here you really have no idea what you are supposed to do with your life. You may think: 'I am stuck and lost'. You may question your beliefs; you may feel unsure of what to commit to.
- Identity foreclosure: Here you may have made a choice, but it was not with careful thought and consideration. You might question: 'How did I get here?'
- Identity moratorium: Here you may be thinking about what your options are, taking stock, doing your due diligence, exploring opportunities and possibilities.
- Identity achievement: Here is the point of realization. You may have clarity about what you want to do with your life, a sense of clarity about your purpose and your plans.

The process is iterative and non-linear. Not everyone will go through all four stages, but they offer a useful structure to explore and be forgiving of your first choices. It is possible to reflect, redirect and make more informed choices about your future work, taking care to think about your values, interests and goals that may well change over time.

Leaping too quickly to an identity without first exploring and experiencing different options and opportunities as a result of societal, parental or peer pressure can prevent flexibility and openness to other options.

My own experience of identity foreclosure happened in my teens. I applied and secured a place to study Economics. I was proud and excited about my future as an economist – how cool does that sound? Yet the shallowness of my attachment to this identity was evident just a few weeks into my study. I disliked the subject. I was not excited by the topics. I did not excel. Luckily I moved quickly from stage 2 to stage 3, exploring options and landing on a course of study in the social sciences that led me to Psychology via Anthropology.

Decision making

Planning our reinvention inevitably involves a degree of decision making. You may have a clear sense of how you like to make decisions – after careful, detailed consideration? Spontaneously? After consultation with trusted advisors in the field of your decision? Or on the toss of a coin?

Of course, deciding to meet someone for coffee is a less tricky decision than leaving a career path you have been on for a decade. Not all decisions are created equal, yet we have a lot to learn about ourselves in the way we respond to requests, opportunities and prospects. Here we will explore the possibilities that the way we make decisions uncovers.

Kahneman and Tversky (1982) introduce the notion of thinking fast and thinking slow, with System 1 thinking offering us the quick, gut reaction and System 2 the more considered, thoughtful deliberative process. This background is useful to consider as we dive into how we make decisions. We will examine this in more detail in the next chapter when we go inside our brain.

Heuristics

This shortcut to decision making (Kahneman, 2011) avoids rational analysis. Instead, there might be a focus on availability: what is the most recent or most salient option? We might succumb to a decision based on a recent news story or the experience of our best friend. Or we may be influenced by authority: someone we respect and admire may influence our choices. So a mentor, teacher or admired colleague may direct us to decisions that we make based on our respect for them, rather than a sound examination of what is right for us.

Heuristics 'can prematurely and permanently narrow one's zone of acceptable alternatives without awareness, offering deliberational speed and reduced cognitive effort at the expense of comprehensiveness' (Lent and Brown, 2020).

The rational approach

This style of decision making suggests that people make rational choices about career, transitions and retirement, based on the utility of the alternatives open to them (Sullivan and Ariss, 2021). This is seen as 'a reasonable benchmark for optimal decision making' (Milkman et al, 2009).

This kind of decision making requires focus and attention. There is a high cognitive demand on the decision maker, examining different variables, potential outcomes and the rationale for making decisions. However, where there is a lot of choice people can feel overwhelmed, and that overwhelm can lead to a kind of paralysis. There are so many options to choose from that the decision maker is paralysed. While choice can seem good and welcome, it does not necessarily lead to efficient decision making.

The plausible path

One response to the overwhelm of a myriad of choice is to select a plausible path for making a decision. We might use a simplifying strategy by filtering out options based on a few of our most important criteria – so we might decide that items on a particular list are crucial. This kind of decision making is known as non-compensatory.

For example, if we are making a decision about a candidate to employ, we might list:

- five years' experience in the field
- three references
- industry-specific experience

Such criteria may help to cut down on the number of suitable applicants, but might also exclude excellent candidates with slightly less experience, those with transferable skills from another sector, or those who have a limited network to secure this number of references.

Limiting criteria can be quicker, but might not lead to the best outcome.

A combined approach

Some suggest that the best way to make a decision is to combine two or more decision-making strategies, so to include, for example, rational, emotional and relational factors, to get the best outcome; a rounded way to tackle the choice we make (Sullivan and Ariss, 2021).

This is supported by research that showed that rational, attribute-based decision making predicted satisfaction and success in everyday decision making, including career decisions (Banks and Gamblin, 2022). This is improved even further when associative knowledge is included; however, participants in this research preferred to go with associative knowledge.

Dr David Gamblin, an organizational psychologist and expert in decision making, offers us a useful summary. When it comes to decisions, rational choice is seen as the benchmark. But people might not do this as it is difficult. Instead, people might simplify based on heuristics, and therefore risk ruling out potentially good options.

This would suggest that there would be benefits in helping people to structure decision-making problems, to assess what is most important to them in a career choice, and to gain exposure to different professions and industries to help broaden the list of options. Rational strategies seem to be improved upon by also including associative and relational strategies – but, again, greater exposure will improve the validity of associations and variety of relational comparators.

Job crafting

There does not need to be a major pivot for reinvention to take place. There might be small, but significant changes. Refreshing your work identity and your career does not always mean changing the organization you work for.

Berg et al (2013) describe job crafting as a means for employees to redefine and reimagine their work in ways that are personally meaningful, where the individuals concerned believe that the work serves an important purpose. This personal meaning influences the meaning of the work.

These small shifts could be:

- physical – introducing new tasks to better suit one's own skills and interests
- cognitive – how one sees and values the job
- social or relational crafting – deciding who one works with

It is not a formal process, but rather one that aligns with personal interests and values, a proactive behaviour by those employees rather than those leading and managing them (Grant and Ashford, 2008).

The difference between uncertainty and safety

When we are in danger it is impossible to think. The blood drains from our brain and goes to our extremities; we struggle with absorbing new information; we revert to old habits and our faulty heuristics. Our ability to make decisions is impaired. So we need to operate within a safe enough environment that facilitates thinking, emotional growth and expression to cope with uncertainty. Some stress is helpful and can be productive, to nudge us out of the comfort zone, to try out our new skills, to venture into new pastures.

But at its worst, when we are stressed for long periods of time we may feel depleted and emotionally drained, in a state of burnout. Our tank is empty and the response to this stress over time impacts our immunity. In summary, we need to feel safe to thrive.

The idea of 'psychological safety' is now understood as a vital component of healthy work life. A psychologically safe workplace is a place of work where it is possible to speak up and disagree without fear of losing your job or being punished. Amy Edmondson (2018) popularized this term, and emphasizes the value of creating a workplace where employees can feel happy and confident that their voice is heard and valued.

But we can also turn this notion of psychological safety in the workplace inwards. Do we feel sufficiently secure to contemplate change and rest with uncertainty? Can we offer ourselves the insight and candour encouraged by psychological safety? Do we have the ability to notice our own limitations and self-imposed restrictions?

A great deal of our working life is driven by a desire for certainty. Are we making the right decision? Will we succeed, or will we fail? Will we be seen as a reliable person? Sitting with the unknown takes courage, to be able to say you are going to try something, even though you are not sure what the outcome will be.

Not knowing

What are the actions you take when you feel uncomfortable with uncertainty?

- Talking (a lot)?
- Making a purchase – soothing yourself with online retail therapy?
- Becoming combative?
- Comforting yourself with food or alcohol?
- Calling a friend who always agrees with you?

Instead, try sitting with the discomfort for a few minutes.

What we cannot control

There are so many variables that are out of our control, we may opt out altogether and question why we would even think about planning. The expression: 'When we plan, God laughs', no matter what your religious beliefs, articulates this ambiguity well. From wars and famine to global environmental disasters, the death of loved ones, love and heartbreak, breakdown and break-through, coming of age, ending of age; we are impacted by so much that is not in our power to change.

Poignantly, not everyone has the secure upbringing that allows them to embrace life with confidence and a belief that the world is kind. We have external events and early life experiences that are not in our control. In many ways the challenges we encounter are not our fault, but much is within our grasp.

We have time to play with. We have an opportunity to think about our purpose. We have options. But when you're overcome with a deluge of options, you need to ask yourself the following questions to start planning effectively:

- What do I want to do with my life?
- How do I want to be remembered?
- What contribution can I make with the hours I am working?
- What is my particular gift to the world?
- What work will make me satisfied?
- How do I want to spend my time?
- What changes can I make?
- What will help me to create the changes that will benefit me?
- What can I do with the life lessons I have accumulated?

It is often hardest to take that first step – to step out of the comfort zone in which we function effectively, recognized as experts, confident in what we can deliver. But much of what holds us back in progressing our reinvention is a resistance to taking that first step.

To move from a place of comfort to discomfort, to try out a new way of being with the possibility of failure or humiliation factored into our courageous decision to jump, we might need to progress one step at a time. We can gently move out of that place of comfort, of utter certainty, to stretch ourselves to try new endeavours, to challenge ourselves, to take on new experiences, moving outwards in this circle of life.

The future of work – can we rely on predictions?

Organizational life will look different in the next five to ten years, and there will certainly be losses. Some suggest that by 2030 300 million jobs will be lost, and AI will be able to perform 18 per cent of the work that is currently done by people (Goldman Sachs, 2023). The same report refers to cost savings and development as a result of AI, leading to a 7 per cent increase in annual global GDP.

But we should remember that it has ever been so. Automation has made jobs redundant, but at the same time created other opportunities. Old industries cast off workers, but new industries create more prospects.

Jobs that we perhaps cannot recognize or imagine now, services that were previously unidentified, ways of communicating, creating security, generating care and contact, will create a need for new skills and capabilities. Our commitment to development and planning for our new futures, however uncertain, will be essential.

Technology is changing and reshaping the world of work, the way we work and the way we communicate, collaborate and interact. The pace of change is so fast that predictions of the future of work must be handled cautiously. Yet drawing on business, academia, studies and literature, we can offer some insights and clues into the way we will be working in the next decades.

A UK Commission for Employment and Skills study into what jobs will look like in 2030 explores the skills that will be in greatest demand at a time of profound change and disruption in work (Rhisiart, Störmer and Daheim, 2017). The study provides insight beyond the UK as we engage in global talent pools, advances in robotics, 3-D printing and AI:

- technological growth and expansion
- interconnectivity and collaboration
- increased individual responsibility
- convergence of innovation
- four-generational (4G) working

The shrinking middle

For Gen Zs and those born post the 4th Industrial Revolution, it is also evident that the kind of work that they may be engaged in in the future is unknown. Regardless of your age, it's possible that your next job hasn't been invented yet. Maybe your next step is to invent it yourself, but what is guaranteed is that your future self will need to be invented too.

In thinking about our work life options we need to be curious (Savickas) and perhaps unconventional (Ibarra). We need to explore, experiment, be open and learn about how we fit ourselves into the work world. Planning is important, but perhaps more important is the work you need to do in focusing on your work hopes and aspirations.

This chapter has encouraged you to question the idea of certainty, to play with possibilities and to question your own thinking as you plan for your reinvention.

REINVENTION STORIES

From table tennis champion to pop star

Zak Abel took to the Windsor stage to perform in May 2023 to celebrate the coronation of King Charles III, in front of a worldwide audience.

A child table tennis star ranked number one in England by age 11, with a gruelling daily practice, his future as a competitive sportsman seemed certain. But as a teenager he wrote his first song, and continued to write as his table tennis career progressed. He posted his songs on YouTube, found a following and was offered a record deal by Atlantic.

Hits and song writing credits followed – but at 21 he was diagnosed with otosclerosis (the bone growth disorder Beethoven is believed to have suffered from) and faced the prospect of going deaf. He had left school with no qualifications to pursue his music career, and he had by now given up table tennis, so this was a terrible diagnosis that took its toll on his mental health.

Fortunately, after successful surgery and recuperation Zak can hear pitch again, and as well as continuing his music career he is also collaborating with mental health charity Calm. He has adapted, recovered and demonstrated resilience.

From pop star to fashion designer

Victoria Beckham is an English fashion designer and celebrity. As Posh Spice she was a member of the most successful girl band of all time, with 100 million records sold worldwide.

Moving from popstar to fashion designer was not an easy transition – the fashion industry is hard to penetrate, even with fame and money. However, her collections have been successful critically, with later commercial success. She is now a well-respected and recognized designer with a number of awards to her name.

Beckham was appointed an OBE in the 2017 New Year Honours list for services to the fashion industry. She also runs Victoria Beckham Beauty, winning Industry Icon of the Year at *Style*'s 2023 awards.

From surgeon to patient and author

Liz O'Riordan, a breast cancer surgeon, was diagnosed with breast cancer at the age of 40 and had a recurrence, thankfully caught at an early stage, three years later. She describes herself as an unlikely candidate for breast cancer – she was a triathlete, fit and well.

She joins many women in wondering 'Why has this happened to me?', even though she knows rationally that she is not to blame – it's just bad luck. Her experience as a surgeon did not protect her from the anxiety of her mammogram or the fear of the cancer returning. Forced into retirement decades earlier than expected (the radiotherapy treatment reduced movement in her arm), she also had to confront the loss of her professional identity, as well as the collateral damage of chemotherapy and its impact on her relationship.

Her platform has helped her and others face cancer, and in 2023 her memoir was published: *Under the Knife: Life lessons from the operating table.*

EXERCISE

North Star

Think of yourself as a lifelong traveller. You are navigating your way through a particularly thick and forbidding forest, when you glimpse a star overhead; a North Star that could lead you out of the forest.

What's your North Star?

Try writing 'My North Star' at the top of a piece of paper, and waiting a while. What will you write?

EXERCISE

Why am I procrastinating?

You know you want to change something in your working life. You are facing a problem. You are in a tight spot. You have hit a brick wall. You don't know what to do.

So you do nothing. This is a decision too.

Think of ways you can disrupt the cycle of procrastination:

- anticipate temptation
- make a public pledge to get something done
- try to break down your decisions into small, bite-size chunks

EXERCISE

Face your fears

- What would be the worst thing about making the wrong decision?
- What would your colleagues think of you?
- What would your clients think of you?
- What consequences would there be for your career?
- What would you think of someone else who made this decision?

EXERCISE

Free writing

This is a technique that allows a free-flowing period of writing that gives you the opportunity to think creatively and non-judgementally about your reinvention plans.

The guidance for free writing is that:

- you decide on a period of time for the exercise (1–10 minutes)
- you write without self-censorship
- you do not show concern for grammar or punctuation
- you write until the time elapses

Here are some topics that will stimulate your plans. Choose a time, choose a topic, and write:

- The thing I always wanted to pursue was…
- The thing that would surprise people about me is…
- Something I always wanted was…
- Something I regret is…

EXERCISE

Identity examination

We looked at the four-stage model of identity development from the work of psychologist James Marcia in this chapter. Spend some time conducting your own identity moratorium:

- Which elements of work excite you?
- What matters to you?
- How important is status?
- How important is money?
- How much time do you want to devote to work?
- Do you want one job or a portfolio career?

You may be anxious and unsure, but what opportunities can you create to allow you to test out your desired identity?

PART TWO

On Redefining Yourself

CHAPTER FOUR

Inside your mind

In this chapter, I'll examine the neuroscience of getting to where you want to be, looking at the beliefs that can limit or free us and the power of self-directed neuroplasticity. We will explore the remarkable power of the brain to change itself, and how our understanding of our minds has developed.

This is a huge topic that could be investigated over a lifetime. Research and extensive studies are being conducted around the world, and our learning is growing exponentially. I'll offer insight into some of these extraordinary advances and how they might impact your reinvention. We will focus on mentalization, mindset, the optimism and pessimism bias and our capacity for higher-level thinking and decision making.

Neuroscience studies the structure and function of the nervous system, the brain and the spinal cord through a biological lens. Psychology is invested and interested in human behaviour and mental processes. Neuroscience and psychology are complementary approaches in understanding human behaviour and cognition.

The two disciplines of psychology and neuroscience have much to teach each other. There has perhaps been some hostility in the past: psychologists viewing neuroscientists as limited, only interested in simpler brains like fruit flies or roundworms rather than the human mind with its complexity and depth. In return, neuroscientists have perceived psychologists as lacking rigour and discipline (Brann, 2022; Prat, 2022).

Some psychologists have suggested there is no real need for us to understand the brain to understand personality or emotional intelligence, questioning why neuroscience is required to understand mind and behaviour (Grant, 2021). While psychologists focus on personality and neuroscientists on neurons, it is evident that both disciplines complement and learn from each other.

We will explore the potential of neuroplasticity to remove the obstacles to reinvention you have consciously, or unconsciously, placed in your mind, emphasizing that it is possible for the brain to flex and change as you too can flex and change.

Yet it is not scientists, psychologists or neuroimagers who will have the greatest impact on reinvention. The most important person is reading this sentence. It is within your power to create change, to adopt a new identity or to take a leap of faith into a new beginning.

Neuroscience is interdisciplinary and liaises with different disciplines. These are some areas of study in this extensive field (Brann, 2022):

- affective neuroscience – how neurons behave in relation to emotions
- behavioural neuroscience – how brain affects behaviour
- clinical neuroscience – an examination of brain function and dysfunction to develop new treatments for brain diseases
- cognitive neuroscience – examining the neural base for higher cognitive functions
- cultural neuroscience – how our beliefs, values and practices are shaped by and shape our brain, minds and genes

- molecular neuroscience – looking at the individual molecules within the nervous system
- social neuroscience – bringing biological systems into the field of social processes and behaviours, both disciplines refining and informing one other

The brain at work

Psychologists often begin their understanding of the brain by looking at the case of Phineas Gage.

Phineas was an American railroad foreman who in 1848 had an accident at work. An iron spike entered his brain, through the frontal lobe and emerged on the right-hand side of his brain. Remarkably, he walked away from the accident. However, while he could function physically he was fundamentally changed. From a well-balanced, shrewd businessman he became uninhibited and profane and with little recognition of social norms. After his accident friends reported he was no longer 'Gage'.

Phineas' head injury led to an understanding of the different areas of the brain that link brain function and personality; how, when there are changes in the brain, there are not just physical and neurological changes, but also changes to the essence of the person, their personality and character. His case was the first to demonstrate that it is your brain that makes you 'you'.

Since the case of Phineas Gage there has been deep engagement in the topic of neuroscience – from the brain's structure to the role played by its different parts: sensory and motor responsibility, language, visual imagery and creativity.

The understanding of the brain, popularized by Paul MacLean (1990) as a three-part structure comprising of the reptilian brain, mammalian brain and neo-cortex (the triune system) is still widespread, but now out of date. The layout of the brain is, however, in three parts:

- the cortex
- the subcortical region
- the cerebrum

Scientists can create a kind of circuit diagram of the brain, looking at connections between neurons. This is called the 'connectome', allowing scientists to navigate the brain in ways previously thought impossible (Mlodinow, 2022). Thoughts, feelings and behaviours can be deciphered – but it is not just about observation. Advances in optogenetics lets scientists actually control individual neurons in animal brains by selectively stimulating them.

Another new technique, transcranial stimulation, uses currents to inhibit or stimulate particular structures in the human brain, without permanent effects. Such developments have led to a new field of psychology known as affective neuroscience.

By exploring our understanding of the brain, we can further explore our willingness to contemplate and to create a thinking environment (Kline, 1999). There are a multitude of brain networks, patterns and chemicals associated with different skills and characteristics. For your brain to be in its most helpful state to achieve your outcomes, you want it to be in a high-performing neural environment (HPNE). In other words, for your brain to be in the most helpful state for your planned activity – this might be problem solving, influencing, resting, exploring creatively, etc.

You will ideally create a different environment for different tasks, recognizing that different neural patterns and networks are necessary to meet different criteria. So if we are fearful, for example, this might not be an ideal HPNE to be creative. Our thinking is likely to be shut down. If we are leading a team, we may wish to create an environment of psychological safety to allow problem solving to flow without fear of coming up with the wrong answer – trust is key.

Essentially, a high-performing neural environment is one that allows your brain to do the work, to do the thinking, to create new neural pathways.

Neuroplasticity addresses our brain's ability to change and adapt in both structure and function in response to sensory experiences. Self-directed neuroplasticity (SDN) refers to our capacity to proactively modify brain function through volitional control and intentional practice. This means focusing our attention in desired ways so that the mind can consciously change the brain.

This is a hugely empowering concept that opens up possibilities to treat a range of challenges such as emotional response regulation and obsessive-compulsive disorder (OCD). Research has expanded to the application of SDN to holistic health communities, for example in relationship and transformation practice (Klein et al, 2019).

In a work context, self-directed neuroplasticity could be used to reduce bad habits such as an inability to switch off from work. A workaholic may introduce small incremental habit changes: for example waiting until after cleaning their teeth to look at their mobile device in the mornings, introducing an 8.30pm cut-off rather than finishing work at 9pm, or charging their phone outside the bedroom to increase the likelihood of undisturbed nights.

Those who work as coaches could be described as facilitators of self-directed neuroplasticity (Brann, 2022). Essentially, coaches are helping professionals who support clients to bring about changes that benefit them. We, as coaches, offer clients thinking space to reflect and reconsider their habits and actions, to help clients to rewire their brains, to do the work of change.

Myths and assumptions

Some neuro-myths are quite fixed in our minds, like the idea that we only use 10 per cent of our brain's potential – which is not true. This is a persistent misunderstanding of the brain. In fact, electrical stimulation of the brain during neurosurgery has failed to reveal any dormant area; even when we are asleep, no brain area is completely inactive.

Another popular belief about the brain is that the two hemispheres can be neatly divided – that the left side of our brain is the logical, rational, gritty part, and the right side the more creative and exciting. While the brain is divided and it is asymmetrical, research shows us that actually there is not much difference in what the brain can do in the left or the right hemisphere.

It is our thinking about the brain that has limited us. There has been a preoccupation with the logical left-hemisphere thinking (McGilchrist, 2019) that has led to an oversimplified classification of brain function. The potential for each hemisphere to work in a multitude of ways is now recognized.

There is a tendency to think that everyone is thinking like us, yet research on representation of concepts, the way you think, confirm that the nature of internal musings can differ. There is an enduring myth that we think in similar ways; the skill of critical thinking, being able to challenge accepted norms and ideas, is not always welcomed in our educational system (Monteiro et al, 2020). The way in which we think and understand our interactions and experience at work is a minefield of misunderstanding and miscommunication.

We may be operating at a sophisticated level in our professional life, yet still stuck developmentally at a much earlier stage of mentalization. Carl Jung brought us the idea of the inner child, the notion that our childhood selves influence the way we conduct ourselves in adult life. Our brains and bodies develop, we become more knowledgeable, sometimes more rational, yet our thoughts and memories from childhood are still present.

So when we face criticism at work, when we fail to win a new client or do not pass a professional exam, rather than responding as an adult we can be activated to respond as a vulnerable child with the associated fear of rejection and abandonment.

A leader may be caught up in their experience of early childhood power relationships. They might imagine, because of their experiences of a dominant parent, that someone not agreeing with you is an insult and a threat to your authority. Early experiences may inform the way relationships are interpreted: we might have learned that making no mistakes was the key to acceptance, for example, and this seeps into the way we treat ourselves and others at work.

Mentalization

The frontal cortex is the largest and most recently developed part of the human brain. It is the reason why the human brain is larger than most animal brains. The frontal lobe is critical for high-level mental processing including language, the ability to link behaviours and outcomes and the uniquely human 'theory of mind'.

Theory of mind, also known as mentalization, is the capacity to recognize that what is going on in your mind is not readily available to those around you. It relates to 'thinking about thinking', and encourages an understanding of people's mental states in terms of what is going on in their minds: their beliefs, ideas, attitudes and feelings.

Very young children, before the age of two, rarely have theory of mind. Their experiences and knowledge and understanding are, they imagine, the same as those of other people around them – other children, teachers, caregivers, siblings and parents. This is famously illustrated by the Smartie tube test. Smarties are colourful sweets that come in an equally colourful cardboard tube.

In the test, a child is given a Smartie tube holding not Smarties, but other objects, like pencils, which only they can see. They are then asked what their caregivers will think is in the tube. If they have theory of mind, they will say Smarties – understanding that their caregivers do not have the information they have.

If they do not yet have theory of mind, they will suggest the caregivers will know that there are pencils inside the tube. The child without theory of mind imagines the caregivers can literally peer into their own mind and have access to the same information that the child has.

This important developmental stage is, however, something many adults still need to work on. We imagine that our colleagues, friends and partners know what is in our mind without us having to tell them.

This can be the source of huge conflict at work – something is very important to us, and we cannot believe that our colleagues or leaders do not see this priority in our minds. We might be doing all we can to show those around us that we are ready for promotion, or skilled in a particular new area. Yet we are not offered other opportunities – we are only seen in our current role and our ambitions are not evident to others.

Learning to communicate our greatest needs and values is vital to successful communication. These matters are too important to be left to guesswork. However emotionally intelligent or smart those surrounding us at work are, they may still imagine that a Smartie tube contains Smarties unless you tell them otherwise.

Evolving understanding

Our understanding of the brain has shifted from a commonly held view that our brains simply got smaller and less effective as we got older, to a recognition that the brain is an organ that is constantly creating new neural pathways; that it is highly adaptable and flexible.

Our understanding of the function of the brain has also become interdisciplinary, taking into consideration mind and well-being. Increasing investigation has also taken place in understanding the role of the unconscious, psychotherapy and drive theory. We will examine the connection between neuroscience and psychoanalysis later in this chapter.

> *We are gradually moving away from a simplistic neural phrenology to an appreciation of the emergence of mind and conscious experience from complex system interactions within and between individuals.*
>
> Cozolino, 2017

The power of neuroplasticity

As our thinking about the brain is changing, we are aware of the incredible power of neuroplasticity. The technology used to scan the brain, functional magnetic resonance imaging (fMRI), not only shows us what the brain looks like, but also provides data about brain function.

With the technological capability to scan the brain, we have the evidence base to see that the brain really can change itself (Doidge, 2007; Prat, 2022). Neuroscientific advances have shown that neuroplasticity does not limit the individual to predefined neural pathways; the brain can be reconfigured and reorganize itself to compensate for loss.

In the complex field of the brain, neuroplasticity can be understood simply as the capacity for the brain to change, to form new pathways and to learn and grow from new experiences, learning and development. This field brings together not just the function of the brain (what we can do, how we make decisions, etc), but also the integration of our emotional selves – how we feel and think.

The process involves three neurochemicals:

- Acetylcholine is released when we focus.
- Norepinephrine brings about a state of alert or agitation. It can also feel like discomfort.
- Dopamine is the reward component that energizes.

So every time we do something new, tackle a task differently, or take on new information, our brains will change. New connections called synapses are formed in the brain and there are changes in our brain tissue. This is magnificent news for reinvention – we have the capacity to change, and the scientific, evidence-based findings strongly support this claim.

Much research shows the importance of our early years and interactions on the health of the brain and the development of personality. *Why Love Matters* (Gerhardt, 2004) and the author's subsequent research (2011) emphasizes the role of a loving and caring environment for the development of the brain. Yet not everyone has a good start in life.

The capacity for new patterns to be laid down is a testimony to our capacity to reinvent. Our less-than-perfect foundations might make that task more challenging, but the neuroplasticity of the brain means that they will not necessarily define us.

THE LANGUAGE OF THE BRAIN

- Adrenaline – a hormone that acts on nearly every tissue in the body and is integral to our fight-flight response.

- Amygdala – almond-shaped and deep within the brain, connected to the hippocampus, involved in emotional regulation.

- Autonomic nervous system – all our nerves, with the exception of the brain and spinal cord.

- Cortisol – a steroid hormone produced by the adrenal glands as a stress response.

- Dopamine – a neurotransmitter involved in learning, pleasure and motivation.

- Endorphins – hormones produced by the brain in response to stress or pain, to blunt the pain.

- Glial cells – cells that maintain balance, form myelin and support neurons, also known as 'the glue', from Greek *glea*.

- Hippocampus – located deep in the brain, this primitive structure is important for memory and learning.

- Limbic system (or the paleomammalian complex) – structures encircle the top of the brain stem and play an intricate role in emotion instincts. Some neuroscientists think this term should be abandoned – see triune brain.

- Neocortex – responsible for higher cognitive functions, the newest part of the brain. Also referred to as the prefrontal cortex or the neomammalian complex.

- Neuron – the core cell of the nervous system, transmits information through electrical and chemical systems.

- Oxytocin – a hormone that produces feelings of well-being and stimulates healing and positive interaction. The 'cuddle chemical'.

- Reptilian brain – comprised of the basal ganglia, suggested to be responsible for instinctual behaviours.

- Serotonin – a chemical modulator with multiple functions, not just the 'happy hormone'.

- SSRIs – selective serotonin reuptake inhibitors, often used to treat depression.

- Synapse – the point at which nerve-to-nerve communication occurs. The synaptic gap is the area between the neuron and the other cell.

- Triune brain – the now-controversial model of the brain that consists of the reptilian system, limbic system and neocortex. Popularized by MacLean in the 1960s.

- Vagus nerve – the nerve that connects the brain stem to the body.

Source: Brann, 2022

Survival and executive functions of the brain

Many of us live our lives in fear. Fear of being found out. Fear of not succeeding. Fear of not having enough. Fear of comparing unfavourably to others. Fear of missing out. When we function in fear, we are operating in survival mode. Our sympathetic nervous system is activated, and we are physically and mentally stressed.

The evolutionary understanding of this state is often related to our ancestral survival in the savannah. When we saw a wild animal approaching we had to respond appropriately; thinking too long about immediate danger would lead to death.

The vagus nerve has a major role to play in our nervous system's regulation. Overstimulation of the vagus nerve can lead to feelings of fight and flight.

We are not in life-or-death situations when we are asked to deliver a presentation or share bad news with a boss or a client, yet our bodies function in this stressed state. Blood leaves our digestive system and is directed to our extremities, our heart beats faster, we sweat – our capacity to think is shut down. We respond with fight, flight or freeze action:

- Fight – when we are threatened by a smart, talented new colleague, we may be aggressive to assuage our feelings of threat. We are literally fighting for our survival, to show that we are worthy of attention and praise.
- Flight – our fear of failure may drive us to never be challenged. We might not apply for a job, leave an organization, put ourselves forward – failure is catastrophic to our survival, and we would rather walk away.
- Freeze – we might have worked extremely hard on a pitch or presentation, but when the time comes, we approach the stage and – nothing. Our mind is blank, we cannot move, we have no idea what action to take. This rabbit-in-the-headlights feeling is crippling in actuality and in anticipation.

In order to think we need to activate our parasympathetic nervous system to send a message to our brains that we are not in danger. That there is nothing to fear. That we are in control. There are simple techniques that we can adopt to 'trick' the brain, including taking deep breaths and using sensory management to deflect panic, allowing us to move from stress to higher executive function. It is here that change can occur; here that decisions can be made.

Affective and analytic thinking

The work of Kahneman and Tversky has brought the two systems of cognition to public awareness. In *Thinking, Fast and Slow* Kahneman writes of two systems of thinking – affective and analytic. Affective thinking is fast, immediate thinking – our reflex reactions to events and experiences, also known as System 1 thinking. System 2 thinking is more careful, reflective, analytic – thinking slow.

Kahneman and Tversky are seen as the fathers of behavioural economics, and their research has found that these two systems of thinking are sourced in different areas of the brain.

Affective thinking is located in the mesolimbic dopamine reward system. This dopamine hit, the feel-good neurotransmitter, makes sense when we think of our desire for instant gratification; the quick high. Analytic thinking is located in the frontal cortex of the brain, the region that controls our higher order thinking and complex reasoning.

Heuristics, or using mental shortcuts, leads us to make quick decisions. This fast thinking can lead to quick but often bad decision making, which can be referred to as faulty heuristics. These shortcuts can lead to some poor outcomes: stereotyping, for example. We need to hold on to the analytic thinking that considers that a typical representation may actually be a more complex pathology.

In terms of work–life decisions we can see faulty heuristics at play – we may, for example, leap to a decision about the benefits and attractiveness of a job because of the high salary, the convenient location or the allure of the brand, only to find that on deeper inspection there is a mismatch of values, a level of dissatisfaction with the depth of the work or perhaps a culture of fear.

The importance of delayed gratification was explored in the famous 'marshmallow test' experiment. Mischel and Ebbesen's 1970 original Stanford experiment saw children given the chance to have one small marshmallow immediately, or two if they waited. This work concluded that participants preferred smaller rewards sooner, compared to larger rewards later.

Follow-up studies tracked the children's progress. Those children able to delay gratification had higher SAT scores, better social skills (as reported by their parents), lower levels of substance abuse, lower likelihood of obesity and better stress responses. This follow-up continued for 40 years, consistently showing that the group who waited patiently for the second marshmallow were successful in life measures. Hence the conclusion that the capacity to delay gratification was critical for success in life.

Many of us, then, would wish to be able to delay gratification. The original marshmallow experiment is powerful and persuasive. However, it does not take into account the impact of the reliability of the researcher: whether they will return when they say they will, whether they will give the child the extra marshmallow as promised, etc.

Follow-up studies by the University of Rochester baby lab (Goodwin and Miller, 2013) exposed the children to a series of unreliable experiences, promising to bring things that they never did, such as better crayons or a selection of stickers. Another group had a reliable experience: the researcher told them that better crayons and stickers were coming, and they got them.

Trust in the researcher when the marshmallow test was later conducted showed that those in the 'unreliable group' rarely waited. Their experience was that the researcher was not to be trusted. The second group with the reliable researcher trained their brains to see delayed gratification as positive – when the researcher made a promise, they delivered on it. So the child's ability to delay gratification was not predetermined, but impacted by the environment and experiences surrounding them.

The suggestion that we can achieve major life changes quickly and simply is something that is feasted upon in the world of social media, marketing and advertising. Transformation can be sexy when sold as something to achieve over a weekend, but in a year less so: the pain of discipline or the comfort of immediate satisfaction.

We are not children in the thrall of marshmallows; however, we might adopt behaviour linked to immediate gratification, not because of our innate inability to delay gratification, but because of our unreliable experience of life. Noting this is the first step in changing our ability and attitude.

James Clear, the author of *Atomic Habits* (2018), urges those of us who are not good at delaying gratification to train ourselves to be more successful with a few small improvements to create a more reliable environment. Rather like training our muscles in the gym with small repetitive movements, we promise and deliver something small, over and over again. This way your brain acknowledges that:

1 it is worth it to wait; and
2 we have the ability to do this

Many of us may relate to the urge to respond quickly to a request or an invitation. I have learned that when I am stressed, I am far more likely to say yes to requests that I would normally decline. A quick 'yes' removes an obstacle from my path. However, this leaves a hurdle to tackle later down the line: a commitment to speak at an event, an article to write that will take up a lot of time and effort. I have learned that a quick 'no' or 'I need time to think about that' serves me much better.

Creating an environment that encourages self-control will help that capacity to pause. So if you are somewhat addicted to social media, leave your phone out of reach. If you find yourself yearning and then buying the latest thing after reading a glossy magazine – stop buying the magazine. Cut things off at the source.

Mindset

The term 'mindset' can be understood as our core underlying beliefs about our intelligence, our capacity to learn and our ability to reinvent. Like other aspects of neuroplasticity, our mindset is not permanent and can be shifted to help us re-evaluate our potential and ultimately to enable us to make enormous changes in our lives.

Mindset change is central to any personal or organizational transformation. We may not be able to control our nervous system, but we can control the way in which we perceive and process events and experiences. We can shine light on an area to create mindset change, introducing new thoughts and small achievable actions, injecting vitality to create a sense of urgency, allowing you to adapt more quickly.

Carol Dweck (2006, 2012) has been prominent in this field, bringing us the notions of 'growth' and 'fixed' mindsets. An educational psychologist, Dweck investigated thousands of children's educational achievements and the link to their belief in the possibility of becoming more intelligent and successful through hard work and determination.

Those students that believed that they could be more intelligent through effort – a growth mindset – put in the extra time and effort, and therefore enjoyed greater success. Her work focused on the way mindset impacts the way we look at the skills we possess, how we face challenges and the way we deal with setbacks.

The way we respond to feedback, the gift that we do not always want to unwrap, is linked closely to our mindset. A fixed mindset is likely to receive feedback as an assault, an attack on the very core of the person, but with a growth mindset this is welcomed more openly as a chance to learn, grow and develop.

With a fixed mindset we view ourselves having certain capabilities and an absence of other capabilities, alongside a certainty that this is unlikely to change. So we might determine ourselves to be bad at taking exams, or writing, or dancing. A growth mindset approaches our abilities and future success in a different way – it is about what we can develop, what we could excel at, what we might achieve with determination, time and focus.

Mindset can be applied creatively to a broad range of world views. It is not restricted to fixed and growth mindsets, but can be applied to beginner's mindset, global mindset, abundancy and scarcity mindsets and entrepreneurial mindset:

- Beginner's mindset – The idea of 'shoshin' from Zen Buddhism guides us to view each experience with fresh eyes, to attempt to abandon our knowledge and experience. This is more and more challenging as you gather years of experience and life. But this state of curiosity and imagination, almost wonder, is a valuable tool in exploring possibilities. Opening our minds to learning from scratch can offer deep insights into the familiar and allow us to ask questions without the critical voice that says: you should know. As a beginner you are there to find out, not to impart knowledge and understanding.

- Global mindset – The global economy means that leaders are working across many different cultures and work practices. What is accepted as normal and welcome in one region is considered abnormal and unwelcome in another. Attitude, style of communication, definition of success and relationship to authority are just some of the potential areas for misunderstanding and difference. A common language for executive effectiveness cross-culturally, a form of cultural agility, speaks to this need for common understanding. So a global mindset considers cultural difference, thinks about the impact of difference, and moves from the parochial to the world stage.

- Abundancy and scarcity mindsets – An abundance mindset is useful in the exploration of reinvention and change. With this mindset there is a firm belief that there are enough opportunities for everyone, not just the one opportunity that exists for the one special person. There are broad solutions, multiple creative outcomes and many routes to consider. A scarcity mindset limits possibilities, creatively and functionally, limiting the solutions open to us (Mehta and Zhu, 2012).
- Entrepreneurial mindset – This refers to the thinking that is constantly looking for opportunity, that is not risk-averse, that embraces challenge and has made friends with failure.

Neuroscientific research supports the link between recognizing the possibility of change and the achievement of such transformation. The brain is malleable and adaptable; with experience and practice connections between neurons can change.

The effort we invest in adjusting our way of being, in working towards reinvention, is linked closely to the belief, the mindset, that potential can be fulfilled, that setbacks are inevitable and learning opportunities. We recognize the possibility of change and development. The research and thinking around mindset essentially reinforces the potential to rethink, to re-evaluate our position, to consider a different way of approaching the way we view the world, our work and ourselves.

Optimism or pessimism?

Optimism, it seems, is essential to our existence, yet we are often irrational in our positive outlook on life. The tendency to optimism is not something many of us are aware of. We might imagine ourselves to be quite balanced and clear-thinking, maybe even inclined to catastrophize.

When asked about whether we consider ourselves to be above or below average as students, as drivers or as performers, we often overestimate our prowess. The Dunning–Kruger effect (2011) showed that people with low ability tended to self-assess positively: a cognitive bias, in other words erroneous thinking and judging, ignorant of one's own ignorance. We also tend to overestimate our own and our romantic partner's intelligence, sometimes by as much as 30 IQ points (Gignac and Zajenkowski, 2019).

Research into this potential bias proffered surprising results: that even when we imagine the most humdrum events in the future, participants tended to glamorize and enrich the experiences with a positive spin.

If the majority of people consistently fall under the spell of the superiority illusion, believing themselves to be more interesting, talented, or intelligent than average, there is a flaw! We cannot all be superior to the majority.

Psychologist and neuroscientist Sharot (2011) explored why it is that humans are wired to look at the bright side of life, often irrationally. According to neuroscientists, it is likely that in imagining your future you will focus on the good things that will happen to you: the flourishing relationships, the successful career, your good health. Could such optimism be a self-fulfilling prophecy – like the label 'clever' leading you to academic pursuit and success, or 'creative' to the pursuit of the arts?

Sharot's research and work claims that the way in which our brains have evolved, to overpredict happiness and success, actually leads to greater happiness and success. Our brains are organized and structured in such a way that our expectations can influence both our perception of what is happening and the way we behave.

The negativity bias is a bias that you may be more familiar with. It is in this mindset that we imagine anything new we try will lead to failure. That a small mistake will lead to catastrophe. That the nine positive comments we received on our work are less important than the one comment that is ambivalent. This bias is the ability we have to hold on to negative feedback much more readily than the positive compliments that we receive, and our likely physical and emotional response to negative stimuli.

At its core, such a negativity bias is a survival mechanism that allows us to learn fast. We will delve more deeply into the propensity for negative self-talk in the next chapter.

The illusion of control

This term was coined by American psychologist Ellen Langer in the 1970s. Its historical reference is the theory developed by Alfred Adler, suggesting that people strive for proficiency and control in their lives.

Essentially, the 'illusion of control' is the way in which we imagine we have more control over circumstances than we do, and overestimate our capacity to influence outcomes. This might mean we attribute responsibility for outcomes that is unrealistic and unreliable. It is also called the introspection illusion. We might therefore overestimate the likelihood of success, which can have detrimental effects, for example if we apply this thinking when gambling or investigating the paranormal. In terms of reinvention and creating change, this can also lead to an unrealistic expectation for our future selves.

We may be under the illusion that if we connect with a particular influencer our product will be snapped up and promoted, or that if we have a coffee with someone we deeply admire that we will be offered a job. This illusion of control is a balance to psychological theory that leans towards the power of positive thinking.

However, it need not be in conflict – acknowledging the potential for the 'illusion of control' can be a useful check point for us. Are we leaping too quickly to conclusions that might be desirable, but are not based in reality?

Neuroscience and psychoanalysis

The father of psychoanalysis, Sigmund Freud, began life as a neurologist fascinated by the mind. He was a rebel of his time frustrated by the divide between medical examination of the mind and brain. He went to study in Paris with neurologist Jean-Martin Charcot, and found a mentor there unafraid of the mind/body connection.

Charcot specialized in dealing with patients suffering with what was termed 'hysteria', and he demonstrated his practice of hypnosis to connect the body with the mind. It was here that Freud observed the clear connection between hidden mental processes and their powerful impact on consciousness.

It is surprising that the fields of neuroscience and psychoanalysis have been separated for so long. Both have a deep interest in the human mind, and the impact of the brain on the workings of the mind has long been accepted. The abyss between psychoanalysis and neuroscience is very much closing (Damasio and Damasio, 2012) with a recognition that Freud's theory of mind was rooted in human neuroanatomy and the presumed neural functions associated with the brain's major structural divisions. The work of Mark Solms (2021), a psychoanalyst and neuropsychologist, highlights that most cognition is unconscious, but that affect is intrinsically conscious – fundamental Freudian ideas.

However, the techniques used by neuroscience – imaging, brain scans – and those used by psychoanalysis – the analytic process – remain very different. Neuroscience deals with the structure and workings of all nervous systems, human and not, while psychoanalysis concentrates on one process and product of the human brain.

The area of neuroscience most relevant to psychoanalysis is the machinery of homeostasis – the state of balance in bodily systems needed for the human body to function and survive. The maintenance of life, however, is not achieved simply, and the complexity of life inside every organism and every brain is where psychoanalysis and neuroscience converge.

Some of the most important progress in the development of neuroscience links to homeostasis: drives, motivations and emotion. The link to psychoanalysis is apparent, but has yet to be fully explored. Progress has been made – the International Neuropsychoanalysis Society has been in existence since 2000, founded by Mark Solms, and there is a journal on neuropsychoanalysis sharing research and development in the field.

> One can see that emerging knowledge from neuroscience is likely to be used with advantage to provide a neural perspective on psychoanalytic questions, ranging from the operation of dreams to the nature of human feeling and interpersonal relationships. The natural alliance will survive.
>
> Damasio and Damasio, 2012

Manifestation and the law of attraction

The law of attraction in its most simple form suggests that like attracts like. That in order to have positive experiences of life, we need to think positively about life. That if we want to have new opportunities, then we must believe that we will have new opportunities, emphasizing the connection between belief and behaviours. Many associations with manifestation are seen as pseudo-scientific, linked to writing such as *The Secret*, a simplified and rather materialistic examination of this subject.

As we have seen with our exploration of mindset, our beliefs impact our actions, and the notion of manifestation is worthy of considering as an element of our examination of reinvention. However, it is important at the outset of this topic to emphasize that many global events, life occurrences and systemic issues deeply influence and at times override even the most positive of mindsets and manifestations. Institutional racism, cultural bias, class wars, gender disparity and financial crisis and collapse can be catastrophic.

Such events, however, should not prevent you from adopting the spirit of this thinking to transform your beliefs and therefore your experiences. With this caveat in mind, let us explore the way in which the law of attraction can be applied in your own examination of reinvention.

Within the law of attraction, abundance is the go-to mindset. Failure, challenges, obstacles and learning are seen as useful in themselves and the key to growth. Here manifestation, or the ability to create the life you want, is within your grasp. You need to identify in detail what it is you want to accomplish or become, to have a positive and clear-cut vision, to have clarity about what you desire.

In addition to abundance and manifestation, Tara Swart (2020) identifies other elements of this positive relationship with the universe: patience, magnetic desire (attracting real-life events to match positive thoughts) and harmony. This is no quick fix; it takes time to lay down new neural pathways, and Swart encourages us to enjoy and trust the process.

Holistic thinking brings mind and body into alignment; being present and recognizing that we do not only live in our heads, but by connecting to our bodies we can regulate our emotions, create greater balance and find strength. For example, there has been a lot of research and talk about the connection between gut and brain, even referring to the gut as the 'second brain'. Indeed, there are multiple neurotransmitters produced in the gut. For example, a huge amount of serotonin (around 90 per cent), the hormone that controls mood, is produced in the gut.

The strong message is that we should not disregard the body. This is a topic we will examine in greater detail when we explore the response to trauma and how our bodies hold that experience – the issues in our tissues.

Whether we are thinking about manifestation or goal setting, identifying our values, or planning our careers, choosing a life partner, or deciding to parent or not to parent, clarity about what you want can be difficult to achieve. We are not purely logical, decision-making creatures and there are many factors at play, consciously and unconsciously, that drive our desire and our behaviour.

If you are not clear about what it is you want, then manifestation is not for you. Perhaps your work is to spend time and energy exploring in-depth what it is you want from work or your relationships, understanding your values, reflecting on your life choices so that you can develop the Socratic understanding; to know yourself.

Manifestation is not a passive process. It is not just thinking about what you want and then waiting for your dreams to come true. It is a deeply self-reflective process of exploration and examination, encouraging you to shed your doubts and insecurities and to focus on the elements of your life that you want to change and create. The core message of this book aligns with this investigation: deciding what you want from your working life, deciding what your reinvention looks like and how psychology can help you.

Brain tease

The brain can be easily tricked. Whether we are actually experiencing an event, imagining an event, or remembering an occurrence, the brain sees this as the same episode (Modell, 2003). The panic and stress we feel in anticipating difficulty or danger creates the same primal response as if the incident were really happening. Our heart might beat faster, adrenaline will course through our body, cortisol, the stress hormone, will be released – simply by imagining threat or jeopardy.

The same thing applies to our brains when we place ourselves, metaphorically, in a calm, peaceful and stress-free environment. It can also be applied to rehabilitation using immersive virtual reality (Buetler et al, 2022). Meditation practice, deep breathing and yoga can all create the change in our bodies that create a visceral change in our blood pressure, heart rate and hormone function.

If I instruct you to not think of:

A PINK ELEPHANT

… it will be hard for you to think of anything but a pink elephant.

Our brains cannot be told not to do something, but they can be retrained.

As we have already identified, many of us hold deep-rooted fears and doubts about our capabilities and potential. We may mask this expertly with an armour of glossy confidence, but not very far below the surface lurks the negative thinking and limiting beliefs that keep us firmly in our place.

Visualizing our hopes and dreams can feel like a risky business. We may edit our ambition, knocking ourselves down before we imagine others doing the same. In this way fear and doubt hold us back: we don't engage in forward thinking with confidence and ambition, because at heart we wonder if we are worthy of such ambition.

Thinking about what you want to achieve without edit, freely associating to the dream job or lifestyle you are hoping for, is worthy of your time and attention. The collage exercise at the end of this chapter might be one way in which you choose to attend to this.

Finally, taking care of the brain

Although the brain has potential to grow and change with each life experience, it does, however, age and becomes depleted. We should be thinking about our brain health, developing our cerebral reserves.

Keeping your brain active, exercising and avoiding bangs to the head will all aid brain health, according to brain surgeon Henry Marsh. We shouldn't take our brains for granted, and we need to recognize its capacity to influence every element of our life: our confidence, our relationships, the way we think about ourselves, our resilience and our purpose. The brain changes when we sleep and during periods of deep rest, so do your best to take care of your sleep hygiene to nourish the learning and growth process.

When we sleep there is a cleansing process for the brain known as the glymphatic system. This system cleanses the brain from potential neurotoxic waste products that accumulate when we are awake, and can take seven to eight hours. It is a paradox that sleep creates vulnerability, yet is vital for our wellbeing and restoration (Hablitz and Nedergaard, 2021).

Try to improve your sleep hygiene by following these tips:

- Allow yourself time to unwind before bedtime – a warm bath, for example, is known to make you feel relaxed and sleepy.
- Leave your laptop and phone outside your bedroom.
- Try to set a schedule for sleep. Set an alarm to go to bed!
- Prioritize getting at least seven hours sleep a night.

Note how much better you feel.

This chapter has gone inside your mind. The potential for reinvention has been examined through the lens of history, neuroscience, the power of mindset and mentalization. We have explored how the brain really can change itself.

REINVENTION STORIES

From psychiatrist to thought leader, author, academic, podcaster and speaker

Tara Swart is a leading neuroscientist, speaker on the global stage, podcaster and influencer. Her work on the power of neuroscience has been captured in a best-selling book, *The Source*, and she works at the Business School, MIT Sloan, where she runs a neuroscience for business programme.

She made her own career leap, leaving the stability of work as an NHS doctor in the UK to set up her own business and develop the glittering career and profile she now has, combining medical knowledge with psychological understanding, neuroscience and spirituality. She is the face of reinvention and creating the change you want through the power of neuroscience.

From a teenager unable to read and write to Cambridge professor and fundraiser

Jason Arday is a British sociologist, researcher, writer and fundraiser. He was diagnosed with autism and global developmental delay at the age of three. Growing up, he did not speak until he was 11 years old. He couldn't read or write until he was 18.

Yet at 37 he is the youngest ever appointed black professor at the University of Cambridge. In addition to his academic success, he has raised millions of pounds for the homeless and children's hospices. He is also a trustee of UK race equality think tank the Runnymede Trust.

His story of perseverance includes a personal goal posted on his bedroom wall in his family home: 'One day I will work at Oxford or Cambridge'. He visualized his future and it became a reality. His capacity to question all that surrounded him, be that social inequality, diversity, inclusion, or his own diagnosis, led him to break down numerous barriers and emerge as a role model in multiple forms.

From pharmacist to film maker, from film maker to transformational coach

Dr Eugene K Choi grew up poor, with a single mother and a belief in the Asian-American Dream. He researched the best paying graduate jobs, and then pursued his degree and career as a clinical pharmacist. By traditional material measures (money, professional status) he was successful.

Yet this did not satisfy his mental or emotional needs. He slogged away for years, but realized he wanted more. He left his stable job in New York and went to LA to invest in a film-making start-up.

This venture did not become the success he'd hoped for. It did, however, teach him a great deal about marketing. Finally, he used his healthcare background to train people in basic neuroscience, ultimately becoming a transformational mindset coach working with entrepreneurs and leaders.

From the UK to AD100 LA designer and entrepreneur

Jake Arnold exemplifies not just the internal vision of manifestation, but the necessary action and drive to reinvent oneself.

Jake grew up in North London and was on track to work as a UK property developer when he had an awakening. Inspired by reading about the power of manifestation, he became laser-focused on living and working in LA. He had no visa, no contacts and no money but a deep belief in this as his destiny. He pursued work experience through Twitter, and landed work as an intern for an LA-based interior designer.

Although an accomplished business graduate with experience working in commercial property, he was an outlier and worked extremely hard to establish himself and gain respect. Studio Jake Arnold is the result. He took a leap of faith and has not looked back.

Jake is now based in Los Angeles and works for Hollywood stars and the glitterati, drawing on his now considerable experience and natural flair for design with his own special take on warm but plush home living. Without formal training, he has drawn on his intrinsic strength to become a powerhouse in his industry, one of *Architectural Digest*'s most influential talents.

He published a book, *Redefining Comfort*, and has a number of collaborations and furniture lines. He has also launched a design platform, 'The Expert', where design consultations take place on Zoom. The psychology of reinvention is at the heart of his work, recognizing vulnerability in the most apparently accomplished.

EXERCISE

For your eyes only – journalling

Our brains are like sieves, and it is hard to retain information, to hold on to learning and even day-to-day experiences. Journalling is a proven way (Meyer and Willis, 2019) to hold these contemplations and experiences, capturing our actions and musings on those actions, as well as frustrations, emotional responses and reflections.

It is also a useful record of our state of mind, a tool to measure progress and a means for greater self-knowledge and understanding (Jarvis and Baloyi, 2020).

I would encourage you to write your journal by hand. The process of writing is more time-consuming and therefore by its nature encourages extra thought and engagement. We are able to mentally connect more fruitfully and offer our personal thoughts more authentically.

You can choose how you structure your journal, but the following headings might help:

Today I had the following:

- thoughts
- feelings
- reactions to life events
- physical reactions, embodied responses

You may also want to focus on development and satisfaction:

- What did I learn today?
- What do I want to do differently tomorrow?
- What has given me pride and satisfaction?

Others like to use their journalling as a means of logging their gratitude:

- What three things am I particularly appreciative of today?

Some people like to rate their state of mind or happiness as a tangible measure. This is something you can do if it appeals to you.

EXERCISE

Collage as a tool to self-knowledge

This is an exercise that can unlock your hopes and desires within a guided framework. It is an iterative process that can be returned to over time and repeated at key moments.

The result is a visual representation of your life, what matters to you, what needs to be attended to and your hopes for the future.

Collect images that you are drawn to and connect to you. These may be in the printed press, magazines, flyers, posters etc. Do not think too much about it, just gather the pictures that appeal to you. Do not edit at this stage; just pull together your collection. Take your time gathering all the images that are relevant to you, both your current and future life.

Group the images together and create a visual board by sticking the images on anything from an A4 piece of paper to a large poster board. You can of course use images that are metaphorical – these can send important messages to your subconscious and add meaning and depth to your board.

Take a good look at what you have produced. Narrate the story of your collage: why have you chosen these images and presented them as you have? What is most important to you? What does the board tell you about your priorities and hopes for the future?

Keep looking at your board; it will remind you daily of your motivation and offer you inspiration.

For more ideas and ways to be creative with collage, see Watts (2022).

EXERCISE

Supporting your vagus nerve

As we identified, the vagus nerve has a central role to play in many parts of our lives, from controlling tension to digestion, from social and emotional engagement to our capacity to deal with stress. It can also be used for our benefit, to support ourselves in highly pressurized situations.

As many times during the day as you wish you can do this exercise to support your vagus nerve, to calm and relax your body and mind:

1 Put both your hands at the back of your head.
2 Turn your eyes to the right and hold them there for 30–60 seconds.
3 Take a deep breath.
4 Turn your eyes to the centre.
5 Turn your eyes to the left and hold them there for 30–60 seconds.
6 Take a deep breath.

If you are unable to put your hands behind your head and want to do this exercise more discreetly, you can take your middle fingers and gently place them behind your ears.

This technique is adapted from Rosenberg (2017).

EXERCISE

The Seinfeld Technique

Productivity advice from the comedy legend Jerry Seinfeld. Guiding an aspiring young comic, he suggested the simple instruction of writing comedy every day, with a big wall calendar to record your progress, each day marked with a big red magic marker to create momentum and reward.

The chain of Xs is motivating, and Seinfeld encouraged the young comic to not break the chain.

Consistent daily action builds results more effectively than a single splurge of activity. In working on your reinvention, you can adopt this technique to allow you to think carefully about your next steps. Create a daily log of your actions that helps you to think, develop and work in a fresh way.

These need not be big tasks, but small, manageable activities that give you a visual of your progress and commitment.

CHAPTER FIVE

The age of reinvention

Age is a factor that can limit a person's ability to embrace change. This could be because a person feels too young, or too old. We might hold in our minds the 'right' time to make a particular change, to take a career break, to retrain, to launch a business or to retire.

This chapter examines the notion of age, and challenges fixed views on when reinvention and new paths can be taken. The key ingredients are not linked to your biological age, but to your desire for change, your self-awareness, your willingness to learn.

The self-limiting belief that directs an individual to restrain themselves because of age is a negative view that can stunt growth and hinder development. We might imagine that we are lacking in skill or experience, that we will humiliate ourselves by sharing our hopes and ambitions. Or we might consider ourselves finished, that our options and possibilities have run dry as we reach a certain point in our working life.

One of the main purposes of writing this book is to challenge the idea that factors such as age limit our potential to switch and reinvent ourselves. Transformation might be different as a Baby Boomer or as a Gen Z, yet at whatever point we are standing, change is possible. There are technical and practical tools and techniques that can assist such a revolution, but much of our capacity to change is within us, driven by our self-limiting beliefs or our out-of-date understanding of ourselves and the world of work.

Essentially, age is just one variable, alongside intelligence, communication skills, emotional intelligence, technical savviness, values and personal ambition and drive.

Whether you think of yourself as too young and inexperienced, or too old and out of touch to take up new opportunities – pause. Your age offers strength and potential for development from wherever you are chronologically.

It is your unique challenge to carefully review what is holding you back – the false assumptions about what is open to you for your age, or how well you will function in an environment that might not typically host your age group. We will look at how chronological age is different to our biological age and to our social age. We can do nothing about the date of our birth, but we can do a huge amount to impact the way in which we embrace and create opportunities for ourselves, no matter our age.

Self-limiting beliefs

We can self-sabotage any aspect of our life and our identity – denigrating ourselves, questioning our right to engage in opportunities, not giving ourselves the chance to participate because we might fail or be a disappointment. This cycle of self-sabotage can limit us in so many ways, preventing reinvention or development with emotional overwhelm that stultifies us.

One popular approach to shifting our limiting self-beliefs is cognitive behavioural therapy (CBT), a rational therapy that encourages you to inspect and adjust your thought patterns. In 1989 the Stanford psychiatrist David Burns wrote *The Feeling Good Handbook*, popularizing CBT. He identified the following cognitive distortions:

- All-or-nothing thinking: such thinking causes us to take single events and impose the result of these on all future events: 'I was rejected from this job application, therefore I will be rejected from all other applications I make'; or 'I was not promoted in the last round; I will never be promoted'.
- Emotional reasoning: here you take your emotions as evidence for the truth. 'I feel guilty, everyone must think I am full of myself for applying for this job', or 'I am not going to say anything at the board meeting because everyone will think I am stupid'.
- Personalization: here we assume responsibility for negative events with little reference to objective facts. We take on the failure, and this is a heavy burden to bear and also irrational. 'The MD is in a bad mood, I must have done something wrong', or 'No-one has replied to my email suggestions, they all hate my ideas'.

Imagine you learn about an opportunity to take on a new challenge. You hear that an organization you have always admired is recruiting, or your colleague is looking for a business partner, or there is a chance to retrain in a field that you have always been passionate about. Self-limiting beliefs would steer you to thinking: my lack of suitability has been established; this is it. Such thinking in relation to age can cause us to limit our options purely on the perceived sense that we are not the right fit – we are too old, too young, too inexperienced, over-experienced, etc.

You think about these events through your internal dialogue, and these internal thoughts will impact how you process the event.

THOUGHT OPTIONS

'That is so exciting and just what I have been waiting for! I am going to investigate.'

'I could make this work!'

or

'I am not the right person for this opportunity, I am sure someone else will be better suited.'

'I'm too scared to express my interest, they will laugh at me.'

The way we feel about these events are created by our thoughts; how you think about a situation will determine how you feel about it. So if our feelings are impacted by our thoughts, if we work on our thoughts we can change the way we feel about future opportunities.

The essence of this approach is that feelings result from messages you give yourself. We need to confront our thoughts to change both our mood and behaviour, doing due diligence on ourselves by really inspecting the way we behave and the way we think.

People are not disturbed by things but by the view they take of them.

Epictetus

Irrational beliefs can include:

- 'I am too old to make a change.'
- 'No-one my age will be taken seriously.'
- 'Because I am young, no-one will listen to me.'
- 'I look too old to work in tech.'
- 'I can't be an apprentice unless I am Gen Z.'
- 'I will be humiliated if I apply at my age.'

- 'My age means I should have become whatever is destined for me already.'
- 'It's too late to change.'
- 'You need to work for years before you try something else, I should stay where I am.'

These thoughts can be deeply disruptive, and we need to challenge them. Albert Ellis developed Rational Emotive Behaviour Therapy (REBT), a therapy that challenges such limiting beliefs and encourages patients to replace them with rational and constructive thoughts.

His work was developed by Windy Dryden, whose extensive publications in the field of REBT encourages, and stresses the importance of, unconditional self-acceptance. He writes of thinking errors that allow us to develop unhealthy beliefs and encourages the development of a realistic view of self. He identifies the following thinking errors generated by unhealthy beliefs, not real-life events (Dryden, 1999):

- Overgeneralization: 'I made one mistake, therefore I am a fool and will continue to make many mistakes.'
- Focus on the negative: editing out positive feedback to concentrate on the negative; the small element of negative feedback drowns out the good stuff.
- Disqualifying the positive: not accepting the positive messaging and sticking to a harsh view of ourselves: they were only being kind or felt sorry for me, etc.
- Mind-reading: convincing yourself people think of you in a particular way.
- Minimization: playing down your success, saying things like 'Anyone could have done this'.
- Magnification: inflating the impact of your errors, imagining these small mistakes will never be forgotten or forgiven.

Most of us will have at some time experienced one or more of these thinking errors. Making a habit of questioning our thoughts, considering if there may be other interpretations, is good practice. The first step is in noting the thoughts that dominate our internal narrative.

Byron Katie has developed a self-inquiry method called 'The Work' (Katie, 2007). Here she encourages questioning and challenging your thoughts and beliefs to help people embrace a more empowering perspective and challenge self-limiting beliefs with these four questions:

- Is it true?
- Can you absolutely know that it is true?
- How do you react when you have that thought?
- Who would you be without that thought?

If we apply this model to the notion of 'I am too old to reinvent myself', or the idea that 'I am too inexperienced to embrace this opportunity', or 'I am simply too young to be considered for this'; we can explore these questions in some detail:

- Is it true?
  - What evidence do you have that you are restricted or limited by your age?
  - What is in your imagination, and what is a result of your experience and knowledge?
  - When have you been told that you cannot apply or participate because of your age?
  - When have you been rejected because of your age?
  - Is this an assumption?
  - Or is it an interpretation?
- Can you absolutely know that it is true?
  - Do you have absolute certainty about this belief?
  - Is it possible that there is another way of looking at these facts?
  - Can your assumptions and beliefs be challenged?

- How do you react when you have that thought?
  - How does it feel to own the thought that you are too old to reinvent yourself?
  - What does this do to your sense of self?
  - What is the emotional and behavioural impact?
  - How does it make you view yourself?
- Who would you be without that thought?
  - How would you feel about your choices and options if you did not hold tight to this thought?
  - What other possibilities and interpretations might there be?
  - What would you be free to do?

Applying 'The Work' to the thought obstacles that you generate can help you move to the place you are aiming for, or at the very least to allow you to give it a go – to step onto the path to reinvention.

NAMING THE GENERATIONS

- The Silent Generation: born 1928–45
- Baby Boomers: born 1946–64
- Gen X: born 1965–80
- Millennials (Gen Y): born 1981–96
- Gen Z: born 1997–2012
- Gen Alpha: born early 2010s–25

Eckert (2017) describes ageing as movement through time, and age as a person's place at a given time in relation to the social order: a stage, a condition, a place in history.

Attitude to career and work expectations varies through the generations, and although it is impossible to make definitive predictions, the following observations suggest some core differences in relation to reinvention.

Baby Boomers are often associated with predominantly one-employer careers, and are seen as an age group that values steady career progression and job security. Career change is a feature of this age group, but less frequent than in the generations that follow, and more likely associated with greater financial stability or development opportunities. This generation is now an ageing workforce, viewed by society and government as both an asset and a problem (Simpson et al, 2012). Terms such as 'successful' or 'positive' ageing are used, as well as 'encore careers' where people choose to use their experience in work that is meaningful and contributes to the greater good of society through a second career.

Gen X are entrepreneurial with a wish to balance work and leisure time and a dislike of micromanagement.

Millennials have prioritized quality of life alongside job satisfaction. Growing up as digital natives, they change jobs more frequently than the previous generation and put great value on job flexibility, holiday time and the potential for working from home for work–life balance. A systemic review of research and data around both Millennials and Gen Z showed this prioritization (Waworuntu et al, 2022).

Gen Z represent the youngest people working, and they are therefore at the early stages of their working lives and careers. They are the first generation to have grown up with an ease and acceptance of the possibilities of the digital age, with direct access to unlimited knowledge and an expectation that information will be easily accessed. They have skill and savviness with technology that has not been taught by an older generation; they are at the forefront.

What research has shown is that this generation places greater importance on working flexibly and making an impact, doing greater good, through their work. Gen Z is also more likely to embrace multiple career changes and be open to pursuing non-traditional career paths. Findings show that this generation has clear expectations and clarity about their career planning (Barhate and Dirani, 2022).

We have yet to witness the relationship that Gen Alpha has to work. In the next decade we can watch and observe how this generation chooses to reinvent the world of work. They will be technically competent, well used to engaging with artificial intelligence and able to observe and learn from the experience and lessons of previous generations.

Age is experienced and understood in complex ways, cross-culturally and through language, for example. Some distinctions are worth highlighting in the context of age and reinvention. We can have different categorizations of age:

- Chronological age – the number of years since our birth, this is a simple calculation provided there is evidence of your date of birth.
- Biological age – our physical maturity, this refers to the way we have aged in comparison to the average or optimal ageing for our time of life. It considers genetics, lifestyle, environment and general health. Our biological age is less fixed than our chronological age.
- Social age – tied to life events such as birth of a first child. Our social age can also be determined by cultural norms, key times of transition and expectations of what implications our age has on the way we work and live. Less fixed than chronological age, social age suggests autonomy to act as old as you feel.

Age diversity is of value at work. Having a mix of age groups offers the space to explore concepts from multiple perspectives, to gain fresh ideas, to offer challenge, to expand thinking and creativity. Of course, there are individual personality and style differences, but the following advantages across the ages can be celebrated.

The advantages of being young as you explore reinvention:

- You are not restrained by years of one way of being and doing.
- You have time to learn and grow.
- You are likely to be tech savvy.
- You are able to transfer those skills to older workers.
- You are likely to welcome collaboration.
- You have energy and enthusiasm.
- You offer a diversity of perspective.

The advantages of being older as you explore reinvention:

- You are experienced and knowledgeable.
- You are able to transfer your skills to younger workers.
- You are keen to learn and grow, to get unstuck.
- You might be tech savvy.
- You are likely to welcome collaboration.
- You have energy and enthusiasm.
- You offer a diversity of perspective.

Ageism

Ageism is a form of prejudice that is often overlooked. Unlike any other form of prejudice, we can all face ageism; it does not discriminate. Ageism is not just about those who are dismissed because they are too old – there is ageism against younger people too.

Some argue that we have not yet reliably quantified the cost of ageism in economic terms, therefore it receives less attention (Levy et al, 2020). However, in October 2021, the first resolution of the Human Rights Council of the United Nations recognized ageism and age discrimination as part of the struggle for human rights.

Workplace discrimination associated with ageing has also not been given much attention (Roscigno et al, 2022). Nor, until recently, has the issue of intersectionality in ageism. Discrimination in other areas such as gender, race, sexuality or disability is likely to compound the cumulative or intersectional disadvantage of multiple stigmatized group membership (Nash et al, 2020). When considering the impact of ageism, it must be considered in the context of other forms of discrimination.

Stereotype embodiment theory (SET), originating in empirical research (Levy, 2009), proposes that there are age beliefs that are assimilated at a young age and reinforced unconsciously. The following three ageism predictors are identified:

- age discrimination: detrimental treatment of older people
- negative age stereotypes about old people in general
- negative self-perceptions of ageing by older persons

Studies have shown a widespread negative view of older workers, depicting them as less adaptable, less motivated and focused. However, there is also optimism in the research. Meta-analyses indicate that job performance does not decrease with age; emotional resilience and innovation continue as we age.

There is, however, a long way to go. A 2023 US study of more than 1,000 organizations (www.SHRM.org) reported that 30 per cent of workers felt that they had been treated unfairly due to their age at some point in their career. Of those, 72 per cent reported that it made them feel like quitting their job. The same study reported that stereotypes remain prevalent – 38 per cent saw older workers as resistant to new ways of doing things, while 49 per cent considered them to be less competent with technology.

Ageism is not restricted to the elderly. Typically, work has been done to shine a light on ageism relating to older workers, but we should also recognize 'reverse ageism'. Harvard Business Review's *Multigenerational Workplace* (2023) cites the ageism that cuts both ways. Glassdoor's 2019 Diversity and Inclusion survey in the US, UK, France and Germany found that 52 per cent of those aged 18–34 faced discrimination, against 39 per cent of those in the 55 and over age group (Gerhardt and Irving, 2023).

Millennials and Gen Z are often labelled the 'snowflake generations' or seen as lazy. 'Snowflake' is used in a derogatory sense, suggesting that members of these generations are overly emotional and sensitive, easily offended and lacking resilience. Just as older generations can be stereotyped as being tech-illiterate, these younger generations are often viewed as being overly dependent on apps and social media, for example to order goods online or get immediate delivery, always chasing immediate gratification.

This labelling, however, minimizes the other perspective of such activities being time-saving. Rather than being lazy, these generations could be viewed as having a different way of prioritizing and using their time. There is devotion to learning new skills, to development and to self-care, to mastering new skills or trying something new – in essence, to using their time wisely.

There has been some research bringing youth studies to the fore, highlighting the focus on ageism against older people and ignoring ageism against the young. Additionally, most research on the young is conducted in the UK and US, while 87 per cent of youth live in developing countries. This has led to this younger age group being labelled as a 'generation maligned' (Kimball, 2017).

Further classification of young people has referred to Millennials or Gen Y as 'Generation We', with Gen Z labelled 'Generation Me' – seeing the former as more collaborative, and the latter as more individual yet with a greater social conscience. All these labels can be reductive, and illustrate that ageism does indeed cut both ways.

In 2023, Keir Mather was elected as a Member of Parliament. At 25 years old, he became the youngest current MP, described in the press as 'Baby of the House', itself an ageist term with associations of premature appointment.

Response to his election was mixed – excitement from some about the impact of youth and enthusiasm, and ridicule and dismissal from others citing his perceived lack of experience and inability to relate to a wider population. He was described by *The Spectator* as an example of 'privileged fuming youths' (O'Neill, 2023), and by *Tatler* as 'the Gen Z MP', 'ready to shake things up' (Bickerstaff, 2023).

Keir Mather was democratically elected to represent his constituency, his passion and vision recognized by the community he serves. Age has proved no barrier. His age at election is, however, surpassed by that of the SNP member Mhairi Black, 20 at the time of appointment in 2015, and fellow Labour MP Nadia Whittome, elected at the age of 23 in 2019.

Mhairi has since decided to leave Parliament, citing outdated working practices as one of her reasons for leaving. It seems that appointment in itself is just the first step in addressing the barriers to age in the workplace.

Am I too old to reinvent myself?

As this chapter has emphasized, the ability to change and reinvent is not related to your age. The global economy is experiencing a talent shortage and many workplaces value mature workers. Indeed, some retirees are coming back to the workplace – see 'Why Britain's absent army are returning to work' (Treanor, 2023). The lure of interesting activity, money, developing new skills and the chance of flexible work are making this return attractive.

The film *The Intern* features Robert de Niro as a 70-year-old intern at a fashion start-up. The 2015 production directed by Nancy Meyers embraces themes of generational differences, age and the value of experience and wisdom in the contemporary workplace. de Niro's character Ben challenges age stereotypes and shows how experience and skill can contribute to success and help build intergenerational bridges. He struggles with so many features of work alongside Millennials – the open plan space, the technology, the pace, the style of communication.

Yet the message of the film is an uplifting one. Each generation has something to learn from the other. The intern adapts and teaches others along the way. The film celebrates the idea that development and growth can occur at any time, and that there is much to be learned by challenging stereotypes of the older worker.

Practical steps to support your switch

In any transition it is important to express your interest, excitement, passion and ideas. Prepare in advance for conversations, interviews and networking events – focus on how you will be perceived, thinking about your energy levels, what you will wear, and how you will share your ideas and enthusiasm.

Here are some reasons why it's never too late to transition:

- Learning agility, the capacity to learn from experience, is a key indicator of leadership potential and learning agility remains constant, regardless of your age.
- There are worldwide talent shortages.
- Companies are beginning to value mature workers – the notion of 'encore' careers is flourishing.
- Experience can give older workers an advantage over younger professionals.
- We should be prepared to challenge those who demonstrate age-related biases.
- Embrace new technologies, consider inter-generational mentorship. Older workers can become tech savvy.

Watch your language

We do not age alone; we exist as part of a cohort who share a life stage or experience. It is central to human experience, 'a continual unfolding of the individual's participation in the world' (Eckert, 2017). Those who have children are often identified alongside a group who go through life together – a parallel experience of life as new parents, school networks, first relationships, jobs, etc.

This can limit our sense of how we experience life. Taking a more expansive view of life events, through our narrative rather than the narrative as a parent or grandparent, can be freeing.

How we describe ourselves and the language we adopt can open up conversation or close down opportunities. If we describe ourselves as 'retired' then there is a finality to that narrative, suggesting a lack of interest in other jobs or opportunities. Instead, talking about now working part time or on a portfolio of interests indicates a move from a particular all-encompassing role, but also suggests possibilities; the expression of interest in reinvention.

Cross-generational perspectives

Many of us hold a perception of ourselves that is not shared by others. We worry if we have a haircut that we think is too short that everyone is looking at us, thinking the exact same thing. The likelihood is that the length of our hair is not something that they have spent any time thinking about. We worry that we didn't know about a cultural reference, or that we got a name wrong, or that we arrived in a dress code different to other attendees, and that we will be judged and humiliated.

As we age we may stress about physical changes: that we are more lined, more stooped, or out of touch. We fear that we will be examined unfavourably. The chances are that others will judge us far less harshly than we judge ourselves, as evidenced by work on social illusions (see next section).

When people transition from one role to another, from student to doctor, trainee to lawyer, apprentice to engineer or trainee teacher to newly qualified teacher, there can be a sense of feeling 'out of place' (Jarldorn and Gatwiri, 2022). This feeling is sometimes identified as imposter syndrome, and can attach itself to younger people. We examined the idea of imposter syndrome in an earlier chapter, but it is worth acknowledging that those who are newly qualified, often younger and less experienced can be prone to such feelings.

Traits such as maladaptive perfectionism and imposter syndrome have been linked with impaired job performance. For example, a study of surgeons found that younger surgeons were associated with less assertiveness and greater imposter syndrome (Medline et al, 2022).

Social illusions

We all wonder what other people think of us. At the extreme, we may have sleepless nights about how we have behaved. Wharton psychologist Erica Boothby refers to such examinations and persecutory thoughts as social illusions. She has explored an idea called the 'liking gap' (Boothby, 2018), examining how we often underestimate the way in which we have bonded with others in social circumstances, imagining we are less popular or liked than we actually are.

No matter what our age we might adopt an over-analytical view of how others see us and be overly critical. We know ourselves inside out. We are familiar with our flaws and our insecurities. We know the ruminating thoughts, the effort we have put into sounding or looking a certain way. We have the full understanding of our fully celebrated and wounded selves.

When we encounter another, they see a fraction of this self. They see the part of ourselves we choose to share with the world, the image we wish to project, the words we choose to say, the engagement we choose to embrace. And yet we often forget this and imagine that others have the capacity to see with laser vision into our very souls. That we will be uncovered in our full, disagreeable and flawed totality.

Research has shown that one of the benefits of ageing is a lessening of the fear of what others think of us. This hypothesis of self-consciousness fading as we get older is being investigated through cross-generational research by Erica Boothby, as explored on the Hidden Brain podcast (Hidden Brain, nd), and by research by Burns et al (2016).

This is not applicable to everyone; certain personality types might not be impacted by our age or generation. Those with a narcissistic personality, for example, are going to continue to think positively and centrally about themselves no matter how old they are. Narcissism does not age.

Yet social illusions are not all bad, and can be helpful in thinking about the times we fell short. We can explore counterfactual ideas about how we could improve, helping us to become savvier as a social actor. It can also be an opportunity to gain a third-person perspective, asking those close to us to give us a point of view on the way they experienced a social encounter.

Letting go of things we can't control in social encounters is something that is celebrated and recommended by the stoics, something we will now explore in relation to age and reinvention.

Stoicism

Let us postpone nothing. Let us balance life's books each day.

Seneca

Stoicism reminds us that life is short, that it is unpredictable. That we should worry about what we need to worry about, not the ifs and buts, or the things outside our control. So when we see a chance to grab a new learning opportunity, a chance to step into unknown territory that might allow us to develop or to potentially succeed in a new field, we should grab that opportunity.

In Chapter 2 we explored the idea of 'memento mori'. This is a stoic concept that should challenge us at any age. If life ended right now, would we be satisfied with the life we have lived?

There are many lessons from the stoics that can support us as we consider our reinvention:

- The world is unpredictable.
- Life is short.
- We should aim to be strong and in control.
- Misfortune is inevitable.
- We can explore hardship and adversity to manage our fear and anxiety.
- We should try to overcome destructive emotions and think, instead, about what can be done.

The 16th century philosopher Montaigne guides us to, in a very practical sense, embrace life now, as in death all our options are exhausted. This is a version of 'carpe diem' (seize the day), which Nike reinvented with its 'Just do it' slogan.

Applying Montaigne's guidance to our plans to reinvent, we should spend time contemplating all the very worst-case scenarios that we fear. If we dare to imagine all these worst-case scenarios, we can appreciate, when not all these terrible things happen, that most adversity is reversible or temporary.

Choose not to be harmed and you won't feel harmed. Don't feel harmed and you haven't been.

Marcus Aurelius

I close this chapter with a reminder of our capacity for self-efficacy. It is up to us to decide if we wish to pursue certain goals, carry out new skills and take control of our environment (Bandura, 2000). The four key elements of self-efficacy are outlined here:

- experiencing success/mastery (it does not need to be big leaps, small steps count)
- seeing others succeed (in our field and our networks)
- receiving encouragement (affirmation for self and others as a powerful motivator, don't be afraid to ask for it)
- managing negative emotions (tackling limiting self-beliefs and developing techniques to challenge your inner critic)

We do not need to limit ourselves because of our age or experience. We can feel fragile when others do not support our ambitions and ideas, when we perhaps do not fit the typical profile of our desired end.

Self-efficacy means genuine belief in our abilities, influencing our motivation to persevere when things are difficult, empowering ourselves and others to believe in our capacity to make change happen.

REINVENTION STORIES

From dentist to make-up artist and entrepreneur

Karen Wagner grew up in a family of medics. Her fascination with the capacity to change someone's face began with orthodontics, and ended with make-up artistry.

With a science-based education, her career spanned fashion, millinery and special occasion make-up alongside raising her family. Her passion for creativity led her to retrain as a make-up artist for film and television.

Being interviewed for a place as a trainee at the age of 45, she was asked how she would feel about taking instruction from someone younger than her. She immediately replied 'I would be happy taking instruction from anyone who knows more than me.' She won a place at a prestigious make-up school and began her career change.

In the early days she travelled long hours for minimal fees to gain experience, but now works for high-profile film and television projects, including mentoring aspiring make-up artists. Her age and experience gives her the capacity to deal with celebrities, recognizing that as the last person to engage with them before they go on set she has a responsibility to deal with both the physical and emotional well-being of the artists.

She further established her position in the field as an entrepreneur, creating handles for make-up bags to allow artists to work hands-free.

From Director of Finance to commis chef

John McCormack decided to retire from his role as Director of Finance of a charity as he turned 60 during the Covid pandemic. He had grown weary of the gruelling schedule of 12-hour days and did not imagine he would return to work. However, soon afterwards he got the urge to work again.

He had taken a professional cookery course as a retirement gift to himself, and found himself drawn to returning to work in a completely different field, as a chef. He now works part time as a commis chef in a pub and values both the development of his hobby into work and the chance to earn.

From CEO to Spanish language student

Kate Davies CBE ran a huge housing association with responsibility for thousands of staff and residents and a multi-million-pound budget. Her career was satisfying and her role full of interest, social connections, power and status.

Transitioning to living in Spain was much easier than expected – the alleviation of responsibility for pace-making for the organization was liberating. There were some losses in going it alone – she lost her supportive PA, for example. Yet living in another country offered her a fresh relationship with a new culture, history and people, and gave her time to learn and grow.

She now works part time as a consultant, using her age and experience to make an impact, as well as continuing her work as a non-executive director for organizations. She also set up a consulting company and became an advisor to a tech start-up. She spent time in Stanford University to learn more about technology leadership and innovation, and is now part of an international group.

Becoming a language student and integrating into a new culture has given her the chance to see the 'Earth from the moon', to have free movement to live and work in any part of Europe.

Where you meet your elders, from the street to the academic office

Dr Ryan Arthur is a lecturer and specialist in learning at Birkbeck, University of London. He shares the experience of encountering a student at a one-to-one tutorial. She began the meeting with the words: 'I am your elder'.

In these four words, the student was executing a power grab. By drawing on their shared cultural heritage, she aimed to reverse the power dynamic, reducing the lecturer and student role to one of elder and younger, where the person of greater age should be given privileged treatment due to their years on earth.

Ryan describes how he almost buckled at this attempt; almost, but not quite. The work surroundings allowed him to hold firm. Had the encounter happened outside the institution he may have struggled more to hold his authority, so deep was his reverence for older people.

EXERCISE

Try one new thing

Part of building self-efficacy is the experience of doing something new and challenging, even when that thing is anxiety-provoking or frightening. Pick a task – you can start small.

If there is nothing in your mind, try one of these:

- Tell someone new about your work ambitions.
- Ask someone to give you feedback on an area of your performance or communication.
- Listen to feedback and say thank you.

EXERCISE

Note what you have learned from past success

In looking forward to future challenges, we sometimes forget those occasions when we have already achieved against the odds.

Recall an occasion when you were proud of your success. What did you overcome to achieve that success?

Remind yourself that you overcame difficulties before. You can again.

EXERCISE

Create a success journal

Make recording your successes, however small, a habit. We often dwell on those things that have gone wrong, the tasks that weren't successful.

Make time daily to note your achievements – nothing is too small. Leave a notebook by your bed, set up a function in your Notes on your phone, put a pad next to your laptop. The key is to remind yourself to note the good things on a regular basis.

Revisit those things once a week.

EXERCISE

(Reverse) alchemy

In the work of David Burns, there is the notion of 'disqualifying the positive'. Here we dismiss neutral or even positive experiences in favour of negative ones.

For this exercise, I encourage you to do the opposite – to use this opportunity to reimagine your negative experiences in a positive way.

Example:

- Event: I have been made redundant.
- Negative perspective: I was responsible for this; if I had performed better, been better, it would never have happened.
- Alchemy: Redundancy is rarely about the individual. I am now able to rethink my choices. What do I want from work? I am fortunate to have time to focus on my next move.

Now it's your turn:

- Event:
- Negative perspective:
- Alchemy:
- Event:
- Negative perspective:
- Alchemy:

EXERCISE

A stoic game

Imagine an instance in which you are feeling challenged. Perhaps you have failed at a task, not been appointed to a job you wanted, or been rejected in some way.

Take time to think about first the very worst that could result from this catastrophe. Then take a more measured view of the challenges you are actually facing.

- The very worst outcome we can imagine:
- The challenges I am actually presented with:

CHAPTER SIX

Leader or follower?

Being a follower or being a leader is not a binary position. Leaders and followers co-exist. You may see yourself through a particular lens, but your experience and role may give you opportunities to function in both ways.

To be a good leader you need to be a good follower, and to follow well requires many leadership qualities and skills. There are very few leaders who are not also guided by another leader, whether that's the board, the CEO or stakeholders. Even those at the helm of world governments, industry and culture take up a degree of followership.

And when we consider being a leader or follower in the context of reinvention, the ability to hold both positions is valuable. We do not need to take flight into one or the other role, but to rest with understanding that we can be both.

The concept of leadership has evolved into a highly examined area of working life. In traditional studies of leadership there is often an examination of leadership styles. We can strive to become charismatic leaders, visionary leaders, supportive leaders, authoritative leaders or participative leaders. There has also been research into the role of a follower (Riggio et al, 2008) unpicking the kind of follower you are, from sheep to star, pragmatist to 'yes' person.

Of course, there is also a huge industry behind leadership development, promoting the latest thoughts and ideas, seeking to reinvent the very notion of leadership. New approaches are sparkling and appealing, and new leaders might also feel that urge to be transformed, to offer something special in their newly appointed role. This adds another level of pressure and demands.

This chapter is not going to attempt to dissect the abundant leadership theories and research, but will instead look at the way we can reinvent ourselves as a leader, beyond the traditional and hierarchical sense of the person at the top of the organization chart. We will look at the thought leader, the self-employed entrepreneur, the specialist, the reluctant leader, and the impact of technology on the way we lead. Reinvention can be from one type of leader to another, from follower to leader, or from leader to follower.

Success in leadership reinvention involves an openness to development, to exploring another perspective, to changing the way we act. A holistic view of leadership reinvention encompasses:

- self-awareness
- emotional intelligence
- authenticity
- ability to adapt

To lead, one doesn't need to be in a formal position of leadership. We can inspire, influence, challenge and guide from any stance in the workplace. Leadership can be a quality that we apply from any position; we don't need to be the head of team to be a leader within the team. We can influence and lead through example and character. In essence, we all have the opportunity to lead.

'Leadership in the mind' is an idea to consider when exploring reinvention. This phrase is borrowed from the Tavistock tradition and particularly the work of David Armstrong, the author of *Organization in the Mind* (Armstrong, 2018). This work refers to the specific way in which individuals internalize organizations – the way they work, the way they connect and what matters to members of that organization.

We similarly may hold an idea, based on our imagination and experience, of what a leader should look like, how they should behave, the way they should prioritize and communicate. This perhaps also needs to be reinvented:

- Do you have a vision of what a leader needs to look like?
- Are you summoning a picture of leadership that is fixed and which excludes you?

It helps to think beyond a single data point and consider the broader picture of leadership. In my work as a business psychologist and coach, I often come across accomplished leaders who are ambitious to achieve more. They want to learn to be better leaders, to be more motivational, to be better communicators, to be clearer in the way they strategize and embrace their people.

The job of leadership is never done – we are always striving to learn more and to develop. This willingness to reject the status quo is perhaps at the heart of leadership reinvention.

Going it alone – the self-employed entrepreneur

Being your own boss is the preferred expression of leadership for many. The dream is to be answerable only to yourself, to be directing, deciding and planning the future with the ability to change course if you so decide. Leading in this way allows you to create opportunities for yourself, to implement change and to be at the helm of every element of your working life.

This brings freedom in many aspects of work, but it can also be restrictive. There is no-one further up the chain to refer to, no structure to support you; the success of the work starts and ends with you.

In many ways, as your own boss, you will also be doing much of the work you might hope to delegate later in your business's development. You are the leader, but also the worker, the follower; it all stops with you: clients and suppliers, business development and execution. You may build a team around you, but nevertheless as the leader you take ultimate responsibility. In some sense, your clients will become your leaders, but without the supportive elements, as their expectations and demands will need to be continuously met and fulfilled. You will need to conquer setbacks, take charge of your emotions and inspire those around you.

The skills of a valued leader will be heightened when you are leading as an entrepreneur – your capacity to create connections, to persuade, to create opportunities and to process and manage the failures that inevitably accompany any new venture.

There are inspiring high-profile success stories, such as the co-founders of Airbnb, Brian Chesky, Joe Gebbia and Nathan Blecharczyk, leaving their corporate jobs to revolutionize the hospitality industry. Chesky and Gebbia had uninspiring jobs post-college, but identified a need for short-term accommodation after Chesky moved into Gebbia's apartment. He could not afford the rent for his own place. At the same time, a design conference held in San Francisco meant there was high demand for accommodation, but few hotels. The entrepreneurs offered bed and breakfast, using three inflatable beds... hence the name 'Airbnb'. Blecharczyk later joined them.

Chesky, as the face of the company, has spoken openly of his failure to secure funding and the struggle to have their business idea taken seriously. Alter (2023) describes Airbnb's 'bumpy path to prosperity', and throughout the ride Chesky has been open about the challenges he faced.

There is a great deal to appeal to entrepreneurial leaders in being free of corporate protocols and red tape, but going it alone comes with greater risk and greater responsibility. The story of Airbnb's success, despite numerous rejections and even ridicule about their business idea, is inspiring – in 2021 it was listed as one of the 100 largest publicly traded companies in the world. But it is sobering to remember that many start-ups fail. Planning the leap and developing a resilience around failure is a key leadership skill for going it alone.

Being an entrepreneurial leader then makes demands on your resilience, your relationship to failure, your capacity to work alone and to develop expertise and understanding across all aspects of your venture. It also brings autonomy, freedom and the opportunity to be truly creative, to form and lead the place of work that is the work of your hands.

The thought leader

Thought leadership can be understood as the capacity to influence an audience by offering a vision of the future, and by providing the action steps needed to get to this desired state. You do not need to be in an organization, or in a position of authority, sitting at the board room table or earning the highest salary to be a thought leader.

Yet being a thought leader brings power and potential: the power to change the way people think about an idea or a product, the potential to influence future action. You can also be a thought leader within an organization, a revolutionary who challenges the status quo and brings new ideas.

This status of radical thinker can equally be applied to those who are campaigning for social justice, environmental issues, changes to the law or even adjustments to the way in which societal norms are accepted by questioning language and cultural practice. There is great scope to be a thought leader.

How can I reinvent myself as a thought leader?

To be a thought leader you need to be able to inspire and influence others by sharing your insights, ideas and perspectives – positioning yourself or your organization as expert and authoritative in a particular field. By its nature, it is a role for the few, not the many.

In order to take up this particular leadership role, we must engage. It is not enough to have original, exciting and innovative ideas that are written down and not offered to a wide audience. Creating quality content that is shared regularly to offer your unique insights is essential. You can be bold; you have to be brave. In challenging norms it is likely you will confront opposition and resistance.

There is a difference between self-promotion and thought leadership. The latter offers expertise in a particular field, to a sector or to an industry. The thought leader does not necessarily need to be charming or likeable; it is about their knowledge and expertise, their willingness to speak up about a subject and to be confident and clear in their arguments. Agreement is not necessary.

A thought leader needs to be prepared to publish on multiple social platforms, run webinars, speak at events, blog, share content and engage with their audience. Being a thought leader means that you will welcome challenge, collaboration or debate; this is the fuel of your expertise as a leader of ideas.

The boss – a hierarchical view of leadership

The idea of a 'leader' used to be understood within a very traditional paradigm – that power rested at the top of the organization and flowed down to the lower levels of the organization structure. The chain of command was clear and usually flowed in one direction, top down. Some long-established and old-fashioned views of leadership rest here, with a big boss sitting at the helm, directing and approving from their position of power, delegating where they feel appropriate. To be a leader in this way brings with it great status and power, but accountability for results rests with you.

Hierarchical leadership, command and control and unquestioned authority were the features of most leadership in the not-so-distant past. An almost blind faith in the wisdom, guidance and abilities of our leaders was not uncommon. Previous generations of leaders were often schooled in a military style of leadership. This has shifted, yet remnants of this view of leadership linger.

Should your dreams of reinvention involve a big desk, unquestioned authority and the ability to wield power without collaboration, it may be worth rethinking your understanding of the modern leader. Traditional hierarchical leadership does still exist, but there is a much greater climate of network leadership with shared decision making, flexibility and empowerment.

The cultural influence of thought leaders such as Brené Brown, in particular her writing on leadership encouraging us to lead with vulnerability, empathy and courage, has impacted leadership dialogue and the move away from hierarchical, command and control authoritative leadership that leaves no room for frailty or vulnerability. The idea that a leader could not express their emotions or seek feedback or acknowledge that they had made a mistake might feel alien now, yet was the landscape of many leaders until recently.

This shift is also fertile ground for learning and development – the notion that a leader needs to know it all is no longer expected. Leaders, like all people at work, are continuously developing, be that in their leadership approach or their understanding and empathy. At the heart of this shift in leadership is the building of connections, of shared humanity and humility and the acknowledgement that we are all vulnerable.

The reluctant leader

There are times when we fight for the position of leader, and times when it is foisted upon us. Some may find themselves in positions of leadership when this is something that they have not actively sought out, nor is it something that they have aspired to. Circumstances have led them to take on the roles that are not part of their ambitions or passions. Their reinvention is not directed by their own ambitions and desires, but by the circumstances they find themselves in; leadership has been thrust upon them.

Authenticity and humility can often be qualities of the reluctant leader. This is not the end of a long game plan, nor a vanity project. This is about duty and rising to the challenge.

There are leaders in history who have been plunged into the position of leadership reluctantly, yet have gone on to excel. Perhaps because of their modesty and lack of presumption, they have worked tirelessly to fulfil their leadership obligations. In biblical narratives we may think of Moses, the shy and stuttering leader, who had the task of leadership imposed on him despite his protestations, or of Nelson Mandela who abandoned his legal career to embrace an iconic leadership role in the struggle against apartheid.

It can be particularly hard to fill the shoes of a founder who has been highly influential on a brand. When Steve Jobs retired from Apple because of ill health, Tim Cook took over. On Jobs' death there was an outpouring of grief, and many testified to his influence and importance. Not easy shoes to fill. Yet Cook has continued to lead the organization, navigating Apple through challenging times and embracing technological developments.

Then there are those occasions when someone's purpose and drive are so passionate and deliberate that leadership is the inevitable path. Greta Thunberg began protesting for action to combat climate change as a 15-year-old schoolgirl in Sweden. Her clarity about human destruction of the planet, and our failure to act to save it, has propelled her into a global leadership role. She has also been a champion in other ways: as an example of someone with Asperger's syndrome which she describes as a 'superpower', helping her to focus, she has also changed the narrative around neurodiversity.

'Why did I say yes?'

A reluctant leader may wonder what they have taken on, and why they accepted the challenge of leadership. They may ask: 'Is the position one that I felt obliged to take as a socially recognized status symbol, or the role that I am expected to take up?' The sense of duty associated with reluctant leaders is a dominant theme, yet we should not feel that leadership is the only option in our desire to develop and grow.

Many teachers are trained to take up leadership positions. Yet, despite having the necessary skills and qualifications, there is a lack of enthusiasm to lead. The idea that the capable leaders are reluctant to become leaders is seen as something of a crisis in many educational systems (Anderson et al, 2011).

The reluctant path is one route to learning and testing our potential, but there are many others, so before accepting a leadership role think carefully. A reluctant leader may, however, become a hugely effective and authentic leader. Their humility and sense of duty may well foster huge respect, trust and loyalty. They may discover resources within them that they had not imagined, and with support they may grow to embrace and love their leadership position.

Purposeful leadership

Leading in a role where we are well paid, enjoy comfortable working conditions, have the chance to take holidays and benefit from a supportive work culture might appear to be ideal. Yet if the primary task of your organization does not align with your personal values and priorities, it can be hard to find meaning in your work. An organization that does not take climate responsibilities seriously, or one that fails to recognize diversity, or prioritizes profit over all else might conflict with the core things that matter most to you.

Michal Oshman (2021) suggests that we may be afraid to identify our purpose. We are so busy doing and working through our list of tasks that we do not pause to think 'What am I really here to do?'. She writes of a duality of fear – firstly fear of not finding our purpose, and secondly finding our purpose but then not being able to unsee it; not being able to act on what we have discovered.

Purpose may drive our desire for leadership reinvention.

Impact of technology on leadership reinvention

The way we lead is woven into our relationship with technology. The way we work, the way we lead and the way we interact will change as technology develops and drives different processes and ways of responding, communicating and delivering. The knowledge, skills and understanding that you depended on in the past are not without value, but ways of working are changing, and we need to recalibrate and refresh our ways of leading accordingly.

As leaders we have the opportunity to turn to different thinkers. We have the chance to overcome resistance to change, for ourselves and those who work with us. We have the chance to adapt and learn.

As artificial intelligence (AI) advances, there is a great deal of potential to reinvent the way we lead, be that making the most of data-driven decision making or utilizing AI to free up repetitive tasks allowing greater collaboration and creativity with colleagues and clients. There is also distrust and fear around AI. Fear that it will cause job loss. Ethical concerns about the way in which data will be used. But it can offer leaders an opportunity to rethink and recalibrate. It offers incredible potential to remove the drudgery from work, and to think inventively about how the extra resources can be utilized.

Leaders do need to attend to the emotional response to AI, the fear that it will take jobs away, that it will mean the end to work as we know it. It is a resource for us to embrace and adopt as part of our reinvention, but a powerful tool that should be handled carefully. We must also remember that AI is only as useful as the humans who interact with it. The information it generates is based on data already gathered, so any bias in the data collected will still be there in the AI response.

It's vital that we use our agency. We must act and use the technology available to us in a way that is ethical and responsible. Human values and the need to align any technological advances with our priorities and ethics is fundamental to success.

Policy makers, researchers and developers in the field are exploring the impact of AI advances. The Future of Humanity Institute (FHI), for example, tackles big questions about human civilization. It is addressing the need for AI to be aligned with human values and scale safely, working in collaboration with key developers such as OpenAI and DeepMind. Together they are researching the governance and ethics of AI, and the moral status of digital minds.

Our leadership reinvention is likely to be influenced by the growth of AI and the way we work with it to ensure it connects with human values may be an important part of our reinvention story. Blind faith is unhelpful – human interaction and analysis is still very much needed.

Specialist, not leader

When we excel at a particular task or craft, progressing in that career can paradoxically mean that you move away from the very thing that drew you to that profession.

There are professions that allow those with passion and talent to develop and flourish in that field. We might imagine the scientist who has no leadership ambitions, but is developing richly in their chosen area of exploration. Or the researcher who focuses on their subject, unencumbered by management responsibilities. Or consultancy firms offering two-track careers, one that allows a focus on clients and the consultancy work, another that encompasses team leadership and internal performance measures.

In my own experiences as a university lecturer, I can relate to this distance. The elements of the job that may be higher status, the title of 'director' for example, come with multiple tasks and administrative responsibilities, meetings, etc. These extra activities associated with the role take you further and further away from the part of the work that I love – teaching and connecting with students. For some, like me, it means a change of direction. I left the tenured academic position, but kept the parts of the job I loved, working as an associate, teaching but not managing programmes.

A different kind of leader

Leadership reinvention is not only about moving from follower to leader, but can also be about reinventing yourself as a different kind of leader, from doing to being. Carrying out the tasks associated with leadership, adopting new techniques and routines, will be part of becoming the leader you wish to be. However, being truly authentic as a leader requires self-exploration, understanding who you are so that you are not only doing, but also being.

Your leadership reinvention can also be a move from a limiting leader to one who helps their team flourish. Liz Wiseman's work on the role leaders play in developing those who work with them is an example of the impact of leadership going beyond the individual. In her influential book *Multipliers* (2010), she introduces the concept of two types of leaders – 'multipliers' and 'diminishers'.

'Multipliers' look to enhance the talent around them, encouraging development and creating new opportunities for those who work for them. 'Diminishers', not necessarily intentionally, lead with the opposite perspective, diminishing the potential of those who work with them and thereby limiting the success of the whole team.

Fox or hedgehog?

The metaphor of the fox and the hedgehog can help us here. The Greek poet Archilochus wrote: 'The fox knows many things, but the hedgehog knows one big thing'. This notion was explored by Isaiah Berlin in one of his most popular books, *The Hedgehog and the Fox* (1953), illustrating the idea that every classification throws a light on something.

If a fox wants to make a hedgehog its dinner, it has many options, including chasing the hedgehog, hiding and waiting to pounce, or planning for a later attack. If you are a hedgehog chased by a fox, you have one mission: don't get eaten. The fox has multiple strategies and can deal with nuance. The hedgehog sees everything through a single view – survival.

The hedgehog on initial examination is a poor opponent for the fox. The fox is fast, cunning, sleek, an apparent winner. The hedgehog by comparison is rather dowdy, slow, perhaps unimaginative. Time and time again the fox tries to trap the hedgehog, and each time the hedgehog does the exact same thing – curling into a ball so that all the fox encounters are the sharp spikes.

These spikes are his only means of defence, but the fox always retreats.

The hedgehog style of leader adopts a unifying single idea, and everything is viewed through that lens. The fox is multifaceted, while the hedgehog has complete focus on a single ambition; clarity about the end goal and a determination to arrive at the pre-defined destination. The fox's options could potentially lead to scattered and unfocused thinking – dealing with multiple issues and possibilities.

As a result, the fox represents creative and innovative leaders, while the hedgehog represents leaders who are regimented and have a clear vision and method. Both have their benefits and drawbacks – neither are any less of a leader.

The manager

Managers are leaders themselves, but they are also responsible for delivering the vision of leaders higher up in the hierarchy. They are expected to set objectives, measure performance, guide those reporting to them and be at the sharp end of getting things done.

The transition into becoming a manager is often difficult. We move from being one of the team to becoming responsible for the team – a different and sometimes isolating role. The social dynamics may shift as, instead of being able to speak freely, we have to meet the expectations that come with a position of authority. Our words and actions have a weight and significance that wasn't there before.

Taking on a managerial role also means that you will be more exposed to judgement, which could be both favourable and critical – at times even unfair. You may be thrown into the deep end, with little time to adapt to your new role or find your stride. In this situation, it's vital that you offer yourself a degree of self-compassion, to allow time to develop your leadership skills.

As with any learning, we need to have repeated experiences of the new skill or ability to ensure these changes become part of the way we operate, of who we are. So as managers we need to establish, and reinforce, the neural pathways of self-compassion. The concept of 'good enough' as brought to us by the psychoanalyst Donald Winnicott is useful here, as it is in so many parts of our relationship with reinvention. Winnicott encouraged parents to veer away from aspirations of being 'perfect' parents, and instead allow themselves to settle with the notion of 'good enough'. He affirmed that in providing the core needs for their child, they were doing enough to ensure their safe and healthy development.

This is an idea that can valuably be applied to management and leadership. There is no one perfect leader, and we can only strive to do our best, to be 'good enough'. This is a liberating idea that can allow us to tolerate some mistakes and slack in the way we lead and manage. Managers can often be so focused on their team and responsibilities that they lose sight of their own wellbeing and self-compassion.

What is important is that we carry out our role without depleting ourselves of every bit of energy and vigour that we possess. This can lead to burnout, and as resilient leaders we want to maintain some reserves of strength for those inevitable setbacks and challenges that will arise.

Leader or follower: do we have to choose?

Do you see yourself as a follower or a leader?

Do you aspire to lead more?

Is your ambition to be in the decisive and authoritative role of leader?

Or do you aspire to be a different kind of follower?

The world of work is changing so fast. The jobs we might have imagined a few years ago might be outdated; the job of our dreams may not have yet been invented. Work in the 21st century is not restricted to a particular channel or style. We may work as a social worker, but also a make-up artist, a lawyer and an influencer, a web designer and a counsellor, a Pilates instructor and a lecturer, a charity volunteer and an advertising executive. We may be a follower in one part of our working life and a leader in another. This notion of a multi-hyphenate identity is not restricted to two roles either – we can be many things in our hybrid work life.

There can be a struggle to shift from the notion of a single-focus working identity. It takes hard work to develop expertise and technical ability in a particular field, to then arrive at a leadership position in that field. Explaining a multiple working identity is likely to challenge work stereotypes, and the outdated guidance and expectations that are still prevalent. We might hold ourselves back from embracing another passion; we may feel pressurized to maintain the hard-won success we have achieved and terrified of dropping the ball, of not giving 100 per cent and therefore failing in some way.

Rather than asking for advice on how to execute those plans, we might find ourselves asking for permission. But we shouldn't need to ask permission to pursue new opportunities or pathways. Rather, we need to take the initiative and step forward with confidence and enthusiasm.

Leaders in perpetual beta mode

Technology has a great deal to teach us about embracing failure and learning from our first attempts. Software development can teach us about the cycle of development and improvement and the notion that we rarely 'arrive' – there is always improvement and refinement to the software.

This is a good mindset for the leader. We do not arrive as leaders when we are appointed; we are a continual work in progress.

LEARNING FROM THE SOFTWARE RELEASE LIFE CYCLE

- Pre-Alpha – the early stages of development when ideas are being explored.
- Alpha – the first phase of formal testing.
- Beta – often tested outside the home site, exploring how the technology lands with users.
- Continuous Beta – continuously being reviewed and updated.

We are learning all the time. Trying new methods of communicating, responding to crisis, dealing with the uncertainty that is part of everyday working life. When software products are in the process of development, they are referred to as being in 'beta mode'. They are not complete, there are still issues to be worked out, still corrections and improvements to be made.

Moving from Alpha to Beta also marks a shift from singular to collaborative work. Pre-Alpha and Alpha work generates ideas; there is experimentation and a building of skills; Beta tests these new ideas, gathers feedback and reflects on what could be improved. Being in a constant state of Beta learning is thinking that can wisely be applied to leadership.

New and established leaders may focus on:

- continuous learning
- self-reflection
- personal growth

We will find ourselves in new positions, with different technology, different personalities and our own changing sense of self and well-being. Allowing the mindset that guides leaders to such Beta thinking can be liberating. We have not arrived; we are on the way.

Why are you waiting?

Are you playing safe? Is your ambition for leadership being suppressed because you don't feel you are ready, or that your skills are not yet sufficiently honed to take on the position of a leader?

Sometimes we are stuck because we don't yet feel sufficiently skilled to leap into a role of responsibility – but most new tasks, roles or positions are challenging. New opportunities and ventures are meant to push us out of our comfort zone, to offer us learning and development. That is why we are interested in pursuing a more strategic role, a job with more stimulation or responsibility. Not knowing it all at the beginning is part of the appeal – we are there to learn and grow.

There may also be below-the-surface dynamics that are at play in your reluctance to make the leap. An unconscious drive to protect yourself, to keep yourself safe from rejection or perceived danger. Many of us fear rejection. Meeting our fears is a way of growing and overcoming anxiety.

The humanist psychologist Carl Rogers refers to the need to confront and work through your emotions (Trunnell and Braza, 1995; Bolton, 2020). He often quotes the line in Robert Frost's 1915 poem *A Servant to Servants*: 'The only way out is through'.

This notion of our fear relating to what has already happened is addressed in the very first issue of the *International Journal of Psychoanalysis*. Donald Winnicott writes of the fear of breakdown, relating to a past event: 'Fear of breakdown is related to the individual's past experience, and to environmental vagaries' (1974).

According to psychoanalytic thinkers, we should treat breakdowns as breakthroughs, rather than fearing them or perceiving them negatively. From collapse, we can rebuild and lead a more authentic life. Perhaps we are being held back by events that occurred long ago, possibly in childhood. Times when we were uncomfortable or threatened in circumstances that are nothing like those we function in now.

Fiona Buckland, an author and coach, guides her readers to 'separate from old scripts' (2023). She encourages her clients to think of transitioning from where they are now to where they want to be in three stages:

1 Separate from where you are now to allow yourself to get moving.
2 Find your bearings and create a way forward.
3 Incorporate what you have learned.

If we apply her separation model to the transition from one kind of leader to another, or from follower to leader or indeed from leader to follower, the first step is to begin to see yourself as having potential in this new capacity, to allow yourself to imagine yourself leading or following in a way that suits you. Work out what kind of player you wish to be, identify and address any gaps in skills and knowledge, and then adopt this learning so that you can embrace your new identity.

When we hit a wall and feel unable to go forward, we can be resistant to doing anything. This sense of stuckness is a topic we will explore in depth in Chapter 7. Perhaps we have not been offered a job after several rounds of interview, or we have tried to get onto a partner selection process at a professional services firm, or our proposals for introducing change have been rejected despite our efforts and enthusiasm. We can feel flat and a sense of loss, drawn to the sofa and inaction.

Julia Samuels (2017, 2020), author and therapist, encourages those who are struggling with the pain of bereavement to just crack on, to take the walk, to make the call, to ensure you are eating a meal or to accept the invite. To just do it. No over-thinking, no deliberation, just action. It is unusual to be headhunted, to be invited to take up a new role; in the majority of cases, we need to seek opportunities. They rarely come knocking at our door.

One of the reasons we are stuck may be our inability to see beyond our current role. We may have blinkered vision, failing to look around at the potential surrounding us. Our frailty may limit our courage. Our memories of labels we have long outgrown may stifle us. We at times need to take the leap of faith, to view ourselves with a different lens, to take the plunge.

Leadership: to love and to work

For some, the idea of moving into a leadership role, either as the leader of your own venture or in taking up authority in another capacity in an organization or place of work, is serious business. This might be the climax of a career trajectory or the ultimate goal of your working ambitions, such that the arrival at this place of seniority may feel both important and solemn. Yet leadership can be fun, it can be cheerful, and it can bring joy into your work and the work of those around you.

> *Love and work... work and love, that's all there is.*
>
> Sigmund Freud

Leadership is the place where these two streams of life – love and work – merge. Gianpiero Petriglieri, Associate Professor at INSEAD, talks of leadership as a kind of love. And as love can take many forms, so can leadership. It can be controlling and possessive, but also caring, liberating and passionate. He advocates for passion and care in the workplace as an integral part of who we are and a need to humanize leadership and work. It takes courage to leave the safety of a role you can do well – to experiment and to play with other concepts and approaches, to become the leader.

A key part of play is allowing your imagination to roam, to consider different possibilities, to explore, to be light-hearted. In this way, make-believe is an essential part of reinvention. We can explore in our minds all kinds of scenarios, outcomes and ways of being, allowing us to play with different work roles and interactions. We can imagine walking in other shoes – our clients, our mentors, those who are working with us.

As we embrace the leader within, we can play and experiment in order to develop our leadership potential.

REINVENTION STORIES

From comedian and actor to global leader

From 2015 to 2019, actor and comedian Volodymyr Zelensky played the role of a high school teacher who becomes the president in *Servant of the People*, a popular Ukrainian television show. In a case of life imitating art, Zelensky ran for the real Ukrainian presidency in 2019, and was duly elected.

Before hostilities and war with Russia, Zelensky took an unconventional approach to politics, vowing to fight corruption and reform the government with the aim of bringing positive change to Ukraine. Since then he has had an increasing presence on the global stage, developing international relations and forging close ties with the Western world.

His communication skills in drama have translated to rousing speeches and campaigning for Ukraine, making him a powerful and remarkable figure. There are other leaders who have moved from creative industries into politics, such as Ronald Reagan who journeyed from Hollywood to the White House, but Zelensky's reinvention is unprecedented.

From private to public sector, a giant leap into the unknown

Jeremy Newman worked in professional services for almost 35 years, as the youngest partner, managing partner and latterly global CEO of a global accountancy and business advisory firm, operating in more than

160 countries worldwide. He was driven and determined to reach the next rung of his career trajectory; laser-focused on his progression.

His approach to work changed after a three-month stint at Harvard Business School, when he began to crystallize his vision for a values-led business. He took those values into his leadership role at a time when such priorities were rare. In his final position before making the leap, he found himself in a high-status, highly remunerated role that failed to feed his soul. He became increasingly concerned with what mattered to him as a person (who he was), rather than the position and red carpet accompanying it (what he was).

And so he handed in his notice with nothing planned; only a sense that he wanted to work more meaningfully, and that the message from the public sector was that those from the private sector were welcome. He gave up the best job his firm could give him, knowing that if he stayed he would be stuck in a lifestyle cycle that depended on his huge salary, despite the lack of other satisfaction.

The transition was not without its challenges. Leaving an organization that attends to your every need, and finding yourself functioning alone, can feel stark and at times frightening, but Jeremy has no regrets.

Since leaving his firm he has taken up a range of roles as chair and non-executive director of public and not-for-profit sector organizations such as the Workforce Development Trust. He has worked as Chair of the Audit Commission and Chair of the Audit & Risk Committee of the Crown Prosecution Service, and in summer 2023 led the UK Government's review of the Civil Aviation Authority.

Even with his remarkable career and communal leadership, Jeremy describes himself as someone with limited self-confidence; an insecure overachiever. His move to a less secure and certain career has paradoxically improved his sense of worth. He is doing work that is meaningful to him.

From Royal Marine Commander to mental health champion and mountaineer

Joe Winch had a long and flourishing career in the Royal Marines, serving all over the world including two deployments in Afghanistan. He envisaged a lifelong career in the army.

While in Afghanistan, Joe witnessed immense horror and suffered personal loss. For a long time afterwards, he continued to perform phenomenally well – his career flourished, he was promoted, he completed two master's degrees, he was devoted to and motivated by those who worked for him. Until the time came that he could no longer function.

Joe didn't immediately recognize his trauma. He adopted the principles that had served him well in the past – to try harder, to work incredibly hard and to devote attention and time to challenges. However, in 2017, 10 years after his first deployment in Afghanistan, he was diagnosed with PTSD.

As a leader in the Royal Marines, he had always encouraged those who had mental health problems to seek help and to speak up. Now confronting his own trauma, he realized that he needed to face his illness and to be open about his suffering, as he had encouraged others to be. His condition prohibited him from living life to the full, and although the diagnosis was tough to receive, he was able to address his mental health and find ways to live his life in a much healthier way: being a better father and husband, prioritizing what matters. Although keen not to minimize trauma, he recognized that there is post-traumatic growth.

Joe now offers an understanding of trauma in the workplace through work in organizations applying the commando mindset, a framework to approach difficulty, using lessons from his time in the Royal Marines. He works with Climb 2 Recovery, an organization set up by veterans that offers climbing courses to help with physical and mental recovery. He is also an ambassador for RMA, the Royal Marines Charity.

Joe is open and frank about the challenges of living with PTSD, and is a speaker skilled at sharing his experience to raise awareness and deepen understanding. In speaking about his own experiences, he is able to open the floodgates to others' suffering, giving permission to name vulnerability.

From magazine editor to cancer charity CEO

Jo Elvin was the editor-in-chief of *Glamour* magazine and then editor of *YOU*, a hugely successful UK Sunday magazine and an industry great. She left this role with its associated security and prestige to go freelance and further reinvent herself as the CEO of a charity, Children with Cancer UK, as well as becoming the host of a podcast, FAME.

Jo has found meaning and fulfilment in another identity. She describes Children with Cancer UK as a phenomenal organization, a charity that will benefit from her skills as networker, communicator and fundraiser – looking at opportunities to modernize the charity and bring value.

EXERCISE

What kind of leader do you aspire to be?

If someone working for you described you, what would be important to you?

What are your leadership values?

Can you summarize your leadership style in six words?

What do you do best as a leader?

What are you working on developing?

EXERCISE

From good to great

The parable of the fox and the hedgehog was incorporated into Jim Collins' 2001 work, *Good to Great*, an examination of leadership. It asked the three questions in Figure 6.1.

In looking at your journey to leadership or your development as a leader, can you answer the three questions?

FIGURE 6.1   Your journey from good to great

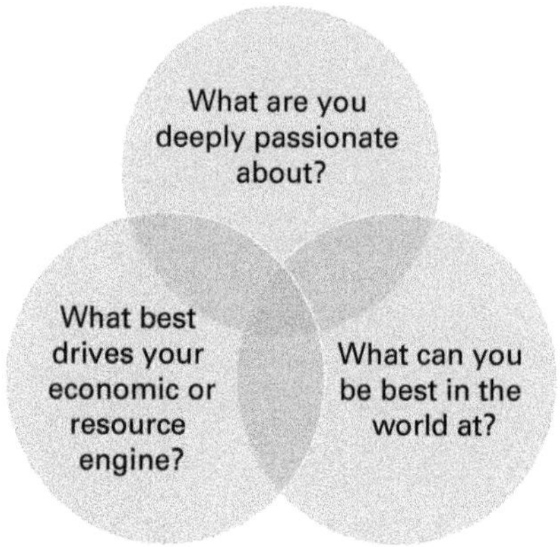

EXERCISE

Your leadership self-portrait

This is an exercise that I do with clients and organizations who are looking at understanding themselves and each other better. I invite individuals to draw themselves and the important objects that represent them.

This is not an exercise in drawing well; it is an opportunity to creatively explore issues of self-identity and the things that are most valued and important to each individual. Colours, materials and resources are available, but not dictated.

Take a piece of paper and allow 20 minutes to draw yourself.

FIGURE 6.2 Your self-portrait

Now reflect on this image. Where are you on the page? What are the most important features that you have identified? What matters most to you? What surprises you? Can you describe yourself and what you have drawn?

PART THREE

On Transformation

CHAPTER SEVEN

From stuck to unstuck

Feeling stuck is common, and it can be internal or external. We may be looking forward, keen to take a step in the right direction, yet we are stuck and somehow held back from moving forward. We might refer to ourselves being in a rut, or having a midlife crisis, or hitting a wall, or feeling blocked.

Imagine yourself on a country walk. The sky is clear, but as the day progresses the rain falls and the ground turns soft. Each step becomes a little more difficult to manage until the ground is so soft and sticky that our shoes are stuck in the mud. We know this is not permanent, that we will extract ourselves, but in that moment we are immobile. We are stuck.

Circumstances in our lives may prevent us from creating change – we may be financially committed and feel trapped where we are, we may be in the midst of crisis and unable to act, we may have family or caring commitments that prevent us from putting our needs first. These factors are tangible and need to be worked through.

There is also the stuckness that comes with our internal beliefs and narrative – the voices in our head that say we can and can't do certain things. These voices may be companions of old, out-of-date voices from childhood or narratives imposed on us by punitive caregivers or unkind figures of authority. These internal machinations can keep us firmly in a position of stuckness. They need equal time and attention in order to free ourselves to move and reinvent.

Perhaps you wish you weren't stuck. Perhaps you feel that being unable to create new opportunities, redesign your life and make changes is a permanent state. Yet being stuck is part of growth. This position of frustration is the first step in understanding what parts of our lives we want to change.

The first challenge is developing from an intellectual understanding of an issue to an emotional understanding. So even when we know all the cliches about change being constant, that it is not rare, and that it is rarely linear, we are still stumped when we are confronted by change. We think of life in stages, progressing from one phase to the next, yet events and changes are often iterative; we move back and forth. Hopefully we learn from the changes we experience, even if at first we are blindsided by them.

Athletes often refer to reaching a plateau. Despite following a rigorous training regime, investing time and energy into their performance, they can see no shift in results. Their personal best is unaltered, they cannot go faster, be stronger, or achieve more, regardless of their consistent efforts. They might feel that they are wasting their time, that they are not progressing.

Yet what might be happening is more about habituation. We all get stuck if we keep doing what we have always done. We need to shake things up, to try something new, to coax ourselves into a new way of being by challenging the status quo.

Research by Adam Alter at New York University (2023) unpicks the anatomy of reinvention. He highlights the inevitability that we all get stuck at different points in our life. We will all get stuck; we need to find ways to break free.

In this chapter I invite you to think about where you are stuck, the obstacles that you need to overcome and the ways in which you can recover from setbacks. We will together create space to confront these obstacles. Many of them may be included in this chapter, but others may be particular to your life and circumstances. I encourage you to attend to them. This is the first step in moving forward.

> The quality of everything human beings do, everything – everything – depends on the quality of the thinking we do first.
>
> Kline, 2015

Here, with these pages as your companion, we have time to think.

Overcoming obstacles and recovering from setbacks

There are numerous ways in which obstacles can halt our plans. We may have daily setbacks that mean our reinvention can be disrupted. We get sick, or someone we care about gets sick. Our loved ones need us. There is a domestic crisis. We confront relationship breakdown, or we suffer loss. Or we receive disappointing news that floors us. At times these are mere diversions that delay or reroute your plans, at other times events cause a major disturbance to your progress.

If you have read with me till now, you will know that reinvention is often an iterative process. We try something, it works or not, we try something else, we go forward, we retreat, we take leaps, we bounce back.

Here we will look at the kinds of setbacks and obstacles that might knock you off course. We will explore being comfortable at work, and our relationship with failure and success. We will dwell on the impact of those obstacles that we cannot escape, like the global pandemic.

Are you embedded at work?

One of the ways in which we can be stuck is ironically through comfort. We have been in our job for a long time. We are known. Perhaps we are liked. There is security and a regular income. We know what we are doing, we are trusted. That safety gives us a cushion to protect us against risk and danger. But it may also prevent us from pushing our boundaries, of being seen differently, capable of other roles, allowed to flourish in different directions.

Is one of the reasons that you hold back from new opportunities that you are established?

Being established in an organization is often assumed to be of benefit to employees. Those who work there are settled, performance has an opportunity to improve, and there is lower voluntary turnover. Yet this experience is not always one of comfort. Research has shown that there are negative aspects to being 'embedded' in an organization. If you are experiencing adverse conditions at work, there can be a dark side to job embeddedness; a feeling that you are trapped, but unable to exit.

A study in Japan and the United States (Allen et al, 2016) supported this notion of a dark side to longer-term employment, particularly linked to abusive supervision and job insecurity. It found that those embedded would be far less likely to quit, but would experience negative outcomes such as emotional exhaustion and adverse health effects.

Can you time travel to imagine another way of being?

An experiment at the University of Barcelona (Friedman et al, 2014) employed immersive virtual reality to generate an illusion of time travel. At the beginning, the scientists invited subjects to identify three decisions or moral dilemmas that they regretted and rate them from 1 to 100, with 100 being their greatest regret.

Next, participants were connected to technology that enabled them to control the outcome of fictional events with tragic consequences. Participants were able to 'time travel' to revisit a sequence of events and change the course of history. Their decisions would directly affect how many strangers would die. The participants were able to re-run and reconsider their actions, to process their moral dilemmas.

The virtual reality experience had allowed participants to change the course of events, to alter history. After this was concluded, the list of regrets was returned to the participants, to revisit their identified misgivings.

Having time travelled, albeit in virtual reality, participants expressed that they felt less regret about their past decisions. They had embraced an illusion of hope that past mistakes could be changed. The past was not immutable.

We do not have time travel at our disposal, but we can employ time travel in our minds. Fear and resistance to change is normal. But if you stayed and stayed, would this be a regret?

Fear of failure

Fear of failure can be a huge obstacle to our reinvention. We live in a world where success is celebrated loudly. Social media offers a constant outlet to celebrate and promote success, and there is a reluctance to share things that went wrong, a climate of almost toxic positivity. This is shifting, slowly and slightly, with podcasts such as *How to Fail* with Elizabeth Day and writers like Joe Moran (2020) who offer solace in the face of failure.

My own work on embracing failure, *Bounce Back* (Kahn, 2019) also encourages a relationship with failure. Failure is inevitable for any life, however gilded it looks from the outside. In most walks of life we can work hard, do all the right things and still fail. Yet we are essentially under-communicating failure.

Failure can also be a vital part of our reinvention. Not every failure can be switched into a success, but it can be our greatest teacher – we learn most from our mistakes. Most creatives, such as artists, writers, poets and musicians, face failure hundreds and hundreds of times in their working life. As Samuel Beckett wrote in 1949, 'To be an artist is to fail, as no other dare fail'.

We have already explored technology developments that are steeped in the lessons learned from failure. Entrepreneurs are constantly facing failure; the start-up may even be described as having 'achieved failure' and mistakes may be celebrated at 'fuck-up nights' where lessons learned from failure are shared. The welcome early recognition of a wrong turn, an unmet customer need or a misjudged market is part of a new venture's evolution. Failure will happen, and we should fail fast.

Academics embrace critical thinking: ideas should be challenged, assumptions questioned. Those who have worked in academia will know that this means developing a skin thick enough to have ideas you have developed, cherished and researched be picked apart and interrogated. It means fundamentally accepting that your passion and work will be probed and distrusted. However encouraged we are to see the critique as collaboration, it can be a painful yet a fundamental part of academic life. It can be crushing.

Successful artists are often prolific artists; there is a relationship between quality and quantity. The idea that we continue to produce, to attempt, to create, to refresh and to move forward is fundamental to our reinvention: we rarely arrive, we are constantly evolving, considering 'What next?'.

Novelist Diana Evans, after four highly acclaimed novels, talks about her wish to be a good writer. She says that the first four books are just the start; we get better and better as we produce more and more. We should do more, as it is hard to know what will succeed. One needs to keep trying. The psychotherapist and thinker Adam Phillips states: 'We share our lives with the people we have failed to be' (Phillips, 2013). Part of our sense of self will be the things that we have not done, the choices we made that cut off possibilities to us, the dreams that were not fulfilled. But this sense of potential can also be an important part of our introspection and fuel action and change.

The end product – the successful artist, writer or actor – might appear to be an overnight success, yet this is rarely the full picture. As actor Sheryl Lee Ralph says in her 2023 TED Talk, 'I do not look like my journey'. Her success as an artist was built on a lifetime of rejection, doubt, struggle and constant drive to be seen and to triumph.

Remembering the mistakes we made, the less polished version of who we present to the world, is important. Not just to recognize how we have developed, but also to remind ourselves that change is possible. In her essay 'On Keeping a Notebook', Joan Didion (1968) encouraged writing things down; something you will note as something of a motif in this book, to allow us to remember, to record our past selves:

> We are well advised to keep on nodding terms with the people we used to be, whether we find them attractive company or not.

A meaningful life means a difficult life. We cannot live our lives without pain, humiliation, disappointment, failure, heartache. As Alain de Botton (2001) notes, there is inevitable suffering in the gap between who we are and who we want to be.

Failure to face failure

The psychologist Lauren Eskreis-Winkler, from Northwestern University, suggests that not facing failure is the greatest failure of all. Failure is often viewed as a teachable moment, yet her findings found that failure undermined learning. She employs a 'facing failure game' in her research (2019).

Her study involves a multiple choice set of questions, but with only two possible answer choices. This means that however you answer the question, you have got the necessary data to gain knowledge and learn:

- If you guess correctly, you know the answer.
- If you guess incorrectly, you also know the answer.

However, her findings across the research sample, be they customer service representatives or general participants, found that people with failure feedback learned significantly less than those who were told they were successful. People with the feedback that they were correct learned in a way that the failure condition group did not, showing a resistance to learning from failure. It seems that failure bruises our ego.

The effect of her study was replicated across multiple domains: professional, linguistic and social. She concluded that failure is ego-threatening, and so we switch off our capacity to learn. We want to be seen as competent, therefore failure is tough to experience.

An interesting further finding from her work is that learning from failure is more powerful when we explore other people's experience, when we are out the way then failure is something that we can learn from.

Failure is telling us something.
It is a gift. At minimum, it is information.
It is up to us to interpret failure.
We live, we fail, we learn and we repeat.

The road to wisdom is through our failures. The idea that we should break down the shame surrounding failure and share our failures openly with a CV of failures was first published in *Nature* by Melanie Stefan (2010). It was picked up as an idea by a Princeton academic, Professor Haushofer, who joked that he became more well known for his failure CV than his entire body of academic work.

When you look back on your life, what are the failures that you note? What disappointments and ruptures did you face? What did you do differently because of these experiences? I encourage you to write your own failure CV at the end of this chapter.

Failure is not always about things that have gone wrong, mistakes made or rejections experienced. It can also be expressed as grief for what we never had and never were (Moran, 2020). This is the motivation for reinvention: we do not want to mourn our unexpressed selves, we do not want to regret the opportunities we did not pursue. We wish to reinvent, even if failure is part of that reinvention.

AESOP'S FABLE – THE FOX AND THE SOUR GRAPES

The fox spied a vine with a beautiful bunch of grapes. Again and again, the fox tried to reach the grapes, but failed. Finally, the fox gave up. Walking away from the vine, the fox turned up his nose and said 'They are probably sour anyway'.

The moral of this tale is that we may disparage that which we cannot have ourselves. In the context of reinvention, it also teaches us that failure can lead us to miss opportunities. The grapes may have been sour; they may have been delicious.

Beyond individual failure, it is worth recognizing that feelings of vulnerability and fragility are universal. Moran cites Judith Butler, who states in *Precarious Life* (2004) that we are largely tender and soft creatures, connected to each other, and we are all vulnerable. We can be wounded or enraptured by the merest glance or nod from another person.

Fear of success

Fear of failure is something that is widely recognized. The association and language attached to failure is well understood. Less examined is the idea of success phobia; in a time when we cele-brate success loudly and publicly an exploration of our fear of success feels uncanny. However, as long ago as 1915, Freud was writing about this concept. In 'Those wrecked by success', Freud notes the surprising, even bewildering, phenomenon whereby a physician discovers that for some people, once a long-cherished wish comes to fulfilment, the patient then falls ill.

A fear of achievement might seem counterintuitive. Why would you fear the prospect of success? Why would reaching your goal be anxiety-provoking? Yet pausing for a moment on this concept, there are many reasons why success may not be welcomed:

- fear of the unknown
- resistance to change
- fear of being exposed and judged
- fear of a loss of freedom
- fear of envious attack
- anxiety about living up to the role
- loss of an identity you have occupied for a long time
- fear that the dream may not be what you hoped for
- fear of being apart from peers and family
- fear of being more successful than a loved one

You may well have other reasons to add to this list based on your own life experiences and psychological make-up.

Fear or aversion associated with achievement is also linked to self-sabotage. Manfred Kets de Vries of INSEAD likens the self-sabotaging individual to a caterpillar that fails to emerge as a butterfly. It does not reach its potential. They possess 'golden larva' traits with the promise of a bright future, but they behave in a way that gets in the way of their success; they fail to thrive.

So we see that success and achievement is not only about skill, talent and potential. It is also deeply ingrained in our attitude to change and belief in our right to take up a new position.

In his book *Fear of Success* (2012), Tresemer cites the story of an athlete, a pole vaulter, finished not by failure but by success:

A pole vaulter routinely cleared 12'6" in competition.

He routinely failed to clear the next height of 13 feet.

This despite his teammates noting he had six inches of clearance.

They conspired to 'help' him.

When his back was turned for take-off, they raised the bar to 13 feet.

Unaware of the true height the vaulter made a successful attempt.

His teammates celebrated.

The vaulter was astonished.

He left the area and never vaulted again.

Procrastination

I'm busy, doing nothing
Working the whole day through
Trying to find lots of things not to do.

Groucho Marx, *Horse Feathers*

So many of us put things off that we know need to be done. Things that are good for us. Things that will support us. Things that will help us to move forward, to create, to develop, to get things done. Procrastination does not apply when the delay is imposed on us by external events outside our control. It is voluntary, unnecessary or irrational, and is carried out despite us being aware of the negative consequences of the delay. The delay is accompanied by subjective discomfort; we do not enjoy procrastinating.

Procrastination is bad for us when it is dysfunctional delay, but delay can also be viewed positively, as in the case of active procrastination (Klingsieck, 2013). Here the procrastinator is fully aware of the negative consequences of the delay, but has decided that there are long-term positive outcomes.

We might need to share disappointing news with a colleague at work, but we delay that event until we have gathered all the facts. Yes, we are reluctant to have that meeting; yes, we are putting it off. But there is thinking behind this. We are doing what we can to create a reasonable outcome. Delaying can be positive.

Stanford professor and philosopher John Perry identified the term 'structured procrastination' in his essay of the same name and later in his book on the art of procrastination (2012). He highlights the important and vital tasks that we can get done, as long as they are not the most important and vital task. We might be reminded of Eisenhower's urgent and important task matrix (Table 7.1). Doing tasks that are lower down our to-do list still accomplishes something; we can still get a lot done.

TABLE 7.1   Eisenhower's matrix

1	2
URGENT/IMPORTANT	NOT URGENT/IMPORTANT
Do these things first.	These are tasks that need to be planned for.
They are the tasks that require your immediate attention.	There is a longer term perspective.
There is usually a deadline.	They might involve preventative measures or personal growth.
3	**4**
URGENT/NOT IMPORTANT	NOT URGENT/NOT IMPORTANT
Things that fall here might include colleagues' interruptions; other people's needs that do not necessarily align with your priorities.	These are things that might be pleasurable, like scrolling on social media or online browsing.
Delegate tasks here where you can.	They are timewasters and should be minimized.

This may be an alien prospect for procrastinators who feel that the best way to address that important thing is to minimize the to-do list, leaving only 'doing the important thing' or 'doing nothing'. 'Doing nothing' often wins.

Perfectionism

As a retired perfectionist, I feel particularly equipped to write about this as an obstacle to reinvention, or indeed to any movement or change. Striving for perfection might appear noble: we want to do the very best, to meet everyone's needs, to be universally liked, to deliver exactly what is needed when it is needed for whomever demands it. Are you exhausted yet?

We can see that the ideal of perfectionism is utterly flawed. It is impossible to be liked and respected by everyone. The beautiful diversity and complexity of working life means that what is joy to one may be painful to another. There is no one perfect solution to anything.

Perfectionism, however, is not always self-oriented. A multidimensional model of perfectionism was researched by Hewitt and Flett (1991), and it remains a useful touchpoint:

- self-oriented perfectionists expect to be perfect
- other-oriented perfectionists expect others to be perfect
- socially prescribed perfectionists believe others expect them to be perfect

All three incarnations of perfectionism can be unhealthy and have an adverse impact on our subjective well-being. Research has shown that self-compassion can help (Stoeber et al, 2020). Throughout this book I have encouraged self-compassion. We are flawed individuals and will always make mistakes; we cannot deliver against every expectation. The kindness and warmth expressed in a caring relationship with another needs to be turned to oneself (Neff, 2003).

There will be no perfect circumstances in which to begin your reinvention. Obstacles of all sorts will cross your path; unhelpful events, untimely loss, health and wellbeing challenges. One thing to release would be your relationship to perfectionism. Striving for a good outcome is healthy and welcome; striving for perfection should be given a wide berth.

The imposter phenomenon

The psychology of self-doubt seems to seep into all walks of life: business, academia, the arts and entertainment. Such thinking is not your friend when you are seeking reinvention. It limits the opportunities we envisage for ourselves and can be unhealthy when we consider other prospects.

When we suffer from a sense of unworthiness in our role, the feeling that we are about to be found out, it creates uncertainty about whether we deserve our achievements or whether we are worthy to be considered for other positions.

Imposter syndrome is often presented as a behavioural health condition leading to burnout (Bravata et al, 2020). This phenomenon has been around for more than 50 years, not always described as 'imposter syndrome' per se, but in other ways such as 'feeling phony'. In 1978, clinical psychologists Pauline Clance and Suzanne Imes identified a syndrome most keenly felt by high-achieving women. They called this 'the imposter phenomenon'. The women they researched found themselves outsiders at meetings, working hard to prove themselves, anxious to perform – embodying the very opposite of entitlement.

The imposter phenomenon is like the enemy within that makes us question whether we are about to be found out. It is the voice that taunts us – we are not as smart as our accomplishments suggest. It is the doubt expressed by Oscar-winning actor Viola Davis, who constantly fights the idea that 'I may not be as great as they think I am' (Davis, 2022). Or that of Tom Hanks, one of our generation's most applauded and recognized actors, who asks 'How did I get here?'; 'When will I be found out?' (NPR, 2016). Hanks talks of his success as a high-wire act.

Our internal misgivings and self-doubt is a subject researched by Kevin Cokley at the University of Michigan. He examines the idea of being 'frauds in our own lives'. His findings illustrate that when harbouring self-doubt, evidence does not disabuse you; we have confirmation bias tied strongly to our doubts. We find reasons not to celebrate, to be our harshest critics and be blind to the brilliance others see.

The imposter phenomenon then can be an incubator for self-doubt, fuelling fear about being overlooked on the one hand, and being found out on the other. Cokley et al (2015) found that high-achieving students were subject to heightened feelings of being an imposter. The stressful and highly competitive academic environment made students feel that they were intellectually fraudulent and phony, putting great pressure on themselves to demonstrate their worthiness, to excel. This is associated with poor mental health, anxiety and depression (Cokley et al, 2017).

Cokley's research pays particular attention to the experience of ethnic minority students, and he speaks of how in his own career as a black lecturer he felt he had to work harder than others to justify his status and position.

Toxic productivity

Many of us can fall into the trap of trying to fit too much into our day, saying yes to things that interest us but that we don't have time for, agreeing to meetings when we have no time to take a meeting, squeezing as much as we can out of a work day. The World Health Organization named workplace burnout as an occupational hazard in its classification of diseases in 2019. This would not have been a surprising finding to many experiencing negative workplaces.

FIGURE 7.1   The cogs of self-doubt

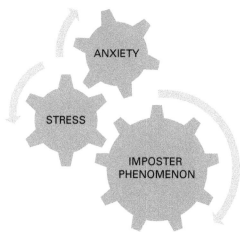

The compulsion we have to be productive sounds benign, yet it can be draining, resulting in the opposite: a lack of productivity and efficiency. The madness of the rallying cry 'Do more, sleep less!'.

An antidote to feeling like an imposter is the quiet comfort of feeling satisfied with who we are and what we have, what we have achieved and our plans for the future. Michelle Obama speaks of her upbringing and her father's message to be satisfied. She describes his words to her: that never being satisfied is what will get you.

Her childhood mantra – not enough, not enough – was explored in *Becoming* (2018), as was her recognition of the need for, and arrival at, self-acceptance and self-acknowledgement. Despite all her gifts and talents, she still questions: 'Am I good enough to have all of this?'.

The hubris/humility polarity

Cokley has explored the idea that internal misgivings associated with the imposter phenomenon can be turned into an asset. As

FIGURE 7.2   The absence and excess of pride

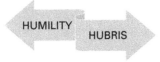

Shankar Vedantam, host of NPR podcast *Hidden Brain*, pithily captures, this is 'greatness driven by the fuel of self-doubt'. The self-doubt experienced by those who identify with the imposter phenomenon drives hard work and a sense of humility.

Those who are touched by this phenomenon are against complacency. But they should be careful not to sacrifice their mental or physical health in the pursuit of excellence. One can be against complacency, but cautious of the cost of proving yourself.

When we contrast imposter syndrome with narcissistic grandiosity, we may see some benefit in the drive and determination to succeed that accompanies self-doubt. Ultimately it is our friend, not our foe.

When obstacles are outside our control: lessons from the pandemic

In 2020, the world faced an obstacle that most had not encountered in their lifetime. It was a worldwide pandemic that paused life as we knew it, and created a new normal from which some four years later we are still emerging.

In these few pages I cannot do justice to the enormity of the experience, but we can learn from our joint experience; we can consider how we got through and the lessons that we learned about who we became after the pandemic. What changed and what remained the same, what we realized was important and what we soon forgot:

- We stopped commuting to work.
- We took our work online.
- We unpacked our bags and stopped travelling.
- We shrank our social groups.
- We put on face masks.
- We contained our lives.
- We taught our children at home.
- We said goodbye to loved ones on iPads.
- We witnessed loss and suffering.
- We turned to our leaders for guidance.
- We cheered our core workers.
- We dreamed.

Terrible and enormous events occur in our lifetime. We feel committed to never letting such events happen ever again. In the 2008 financial crash, the financial industry vowed to never let greed and hubris run the sector. Yet how many lessons have been learned? The boom-and-bust cycle repeats itself, as Freud predicted in his work on the compulsion to repeat (Kahn, 2017). We witness great suffering, genocide, war, cruelty, and in the midst of the pain vow that such suffering must never, never happen again. It does.

During lockdown we cheered for our key workers, in the UK we clapped for our National Health Service. We congratulated ourselves on recognizing what really counts in this world: care, love, our health. Newspaper columns were written in praise of our medical heroes; poetry was published in celebration of those on the frontline:

> We are shaking and breaking and waking indifference.
> We are quaking and taking and making a difference.
> (Lemn Sissay, 'Making a Difference' (in Alma and Amiel, 2020))

But how quickly we forget. Not those who have lost loved ones or suffered working conditions that took them to dark, dark places. But for most of us, we move on. This is our resilience, but it is also a reminder of how hard we need to work to remember the lessons of adversity.

This may sound rather bleak when we're talking of reinvention, but the message of such events is stark. We need to keep remembering and holding at the front of our minds the lessons from these occurrences. It is not enough to witness them in the moment. We need to make lasting change.

When you experience intolerable treatment at work, when you feel undervalued, when you know you are worth more than the way you are living your life, you need to hold on tight to that, to allow it to drive you to make changes. To not accept the unacceptable. To strive for better for yourself.

REINVENTION STORIES

From life without limbs to life without limits

Nick Vujicic is the founder of the not-for-profit organization Life Without Limbs. He was born with a rare congenital disorder, Tetra-Amelia syndrome. This condition left him without arms or legs, and the associated physical and emotional challenges associated with this.

At the age of 17 he gave his first speech, and from this experience went on to find a platform to share his message of hope and purpose. He experienced bullying, considered suicide, and used his experiences to share his wisdom about the power of words.

His faith is central to his message. His TED Talk has been watched by millions.

From captive to advocate

Elizabeth Smart was 14 when she was kidnapped from her family home in Salt Lake City, Utah, and held hostage for nine months. Her experience was traumatic and might have led to collapse and retreat.

Instead, she became an advocate for missing persons and survivors of abduction and sexual assault. She used interest in her personal story to create a platform and support legislation protecting children from abuse and exploitation, reporting that her family and faith gave her resilience.

She established a foundation, campaigned for women's self-defence and has been a spokesperson for survivors of sexual assault. In addition to her advocacy work, she has written books about her experience aimed at supporting survivors of trauma.

A decade of 'no' before self-belief

Sheryl Lee Ralph won an Emmy award for best supporting actress in 2022. She speaks of her many moments of doubt and disbelief, and her drive to continue despite multiple rejections and disappointments. When mental, physical, social and climate demands are creating mental health challenges, she proposes we need 'a check-up from the neck up' – a reframing of our ability to believe in ourselves.

After a childhood of bullying and isolation as the only black student at her school, she was supported by strong parents. Her mother guided her: every negative thing said to you bounces off you and sticks to them, you are rubber and they are glue. Her father taught her to think.

In the world of Hollywood, and elsewhere, she implores us to act like we believe in ourselves, as she shares in her 2023 TED Talk. Look in the mirror and love what you see, or at least respect, encourage and empower it.

From teenage footballer to global history-maker

Jake Daniels is the first active male professional footballer to come out as gay in more than three decades. He did so to overnight global acclaim, in contrast to the hostility and homophobic abuse endured by his predecessor Justin Fashanu who tragically took his own life after coming out in the 1990s.

Daniels's story is not one of unburdening himself from a closeted and secret life. He announced his sexuality in order to be authentic and able to live his life. His reinvention is one that reaches beyond his personal sexuality, and opens the door to transformation for many other gay footballers living with homophobia.

He has spoken out about the government and the Football Association (FA), a young and talented footballer who has transformed himself into a campaigner and role model.

EXERCISE

Check your toxic productivity

There is a narrative that can be hard to ignore that says in order to be successful and worthwhile, we must push ourselves to work hard, to deliver long hours and channel all our energy into work. Yet overworking can be a habit we form that has the opposite effect. Are you aware of this drive to be hyper-productive?

Answer the following questions to test your own relationship with toxic productivity. If you see yourself in these questions, it is time to press pause, to check your current behaviour and work to become more healthily productive:

- Do you feel that you are not doing enough?
- Do you measure your success based on the number of hours you work?
- Do you find you work hours that mean that you rarely have down time?
- Do you take a break after a few hours of work?
- Do you check your phone at mealtimes?
- Do you get seven hours of sleep?
- Do you take a day off during the week?
- Do you eat regularly?
- Do you feel fatigued?
- Do you feel anxious?
- Do you schedule short breaks between your meetings?

EXERCISE

Remember your accomplishments

It is easy to forget in a busy life that the small successes are worthy of note. It is easy to marginalize our accomplishments.

Be intentional about documenting your successes by creating a work diary of your accomplishments. Note down everything that you have achieved, no matter how small.

Over time, you will build a stock of success that will boost you when self-doubt creeps in.

EXERCISE

Failure CV

In 2016, Professor Johannes Haushofer published a CV with a difference. Instead of highlighting his achievements and publications, he listed all his rejections: funding he didn't receive, projects that failed. He did this in an attempt to address the balance of visibility – most failures are invisible, whereas successes are public.

It received much attention and much praise. Haushofer jokes that this CV of failures has received more attention than his entire body of academic work.

Write your own CV of failures, with the associated learning from these:

- Did they spur you on to learn more, or behave differently?
- Did you move on to work in another way?
- Did you reinvent yourself because of these failures?

FIGURE 7.3 Lessons from failure

Lessons I learned	Jobs you didn't get
What I learned about myself – my strengths, where I need to develop	Promotions you weren't awarded
What action did that inspire?	Business ideas that failed
Did this make me rethink my role?	Performance reviews that disappointed

EXERCISE

Are you a procrastinator?

You can use Eisenhower's matrix to help you prioritize the things that really must be done. First, make a list of everything you wish to accomplish. Then allocate these tasks to one of the four quadrants:

- Do tasks in quadrant 1 first.
- Schedule time for tasks in quadrant 2.
- Is there a way to delegate the tasks in quadrant 3?
- Try to eliminate items in quadrant 4 or save them for your leisure time.

1 URGENT/IMPORTANT	2 NOT URGENT/IMPORTANT
3 URGENT/NOT IMPORTANT	4 NOT URGENT/NOT IMPORTANT

EXERCISE

An exercise in self-compassion

You are invited to take a self-compassion break (Neff, 2003).

First, call to mind something that is causing you difficulty in your life, something that is making you feel stressed. Rest your mind in that difficult place, and see if you can experience the discomfort and emotional distress in your body.

You may feel self-conscious about expressing this, but name your hurt and stress. You are not alone; everyone struggles with difficulties. Say to yourself: 'This is a moment of suffering'. Suffering is a part of life.

Put your hands over your heart. Feel the warmth of your hands on your chest. Then say to yourself: 'May I be kind to myself' or another phrase that is meaningful to you; perhaps: 'May I be strong'; 'May I forgive myself'; 'May I be patient'; 'May I accept myself as I am'.

You can do this exercise at any time to soothe yourself and to increase your understanding and self-compassion.

EXERCISE

A conversation with your inner critic

We all have voices in our head; narratives that we repeat and turn to in situations outside the norm. Some of these voices may be benign and kind; many are likely to be judgemental and harsh. If you feel your inner critic encroaching on your time, try this simple exercise.

Invite your inner critic to leave you in peace for a short while. You are not denying the existence of this critical inner voice – that is there – but you are asking the voice to be quiet while you get on.

Say to your inner critic: 'Please step outside while I work. I know you are there, but I would appreciate you letting me get on with this – you can return later.'

CHAPTER EIGHT

Build your support network

Embarking on change can feel daunting, and it can feel lonely. We are social creatures that benefit from the stimulation and support of people we trust around us. In the field of positive psychology, social relationships are deemed to be the most important predictor of people's wellbeing. Without these relationships people cannot maximize their well-being (Baumeister and Leary, 2017; Dunbar and Shultz, 2007).

This chapter explores the ways in which you can build a tribe around you to support you. Some of these people may already be firmly in place, others may be strangers. We will look at the different options you have to build your support network and to embark on your journey to your new self.

The challenge of social isolation

What makes us happy is often the time spent with those we trust and feel affection for. Gillian Sandstrom, a psychologist who describes herself as very shy, researches the value of social interaction. She distinguishes between those with whom we have strong ties (family, friends, close colleagues) and those we interact with where we have weak ties – mutual familiarity, but no established relationship (the barista in our local coffee shop or the Uber driver). Our daily interaction with a wide range of people has been much less studied than the interactions with close friends and family. Research, however, highlights the power of weak ties, those looser contacts who contribute to our broader well-being (Sandstrom and Dunn, 2014). This is powerful evidence for building our network.

Sandstrom notes a paradox whereby we avoid talking to those who are not in our immediate circle, even though doing so will make us happier. We fear that an interaction with someone we don't know will be threatening or uncomfortable (Sandstrom and Boothby, 2021). This venturing outside of our comfortable circle of trusted friends and family is similar to the exploration of learning and our comfort zones that we examined in Chapter 3. It feels safer to stay where we are, to know where conversations might take us, to be soothed by the expected.

But living in an echo chamber of shared experiences and dialogue limits us. We are not pushed to think differently, to use our imaginations or to find ourselves in a position of ignorance but with an urge to find out more.

It can feel risky to begin a conversation with someone we do not know. We might be concerned about how we come across; whether we are seen as over-friendly, or needy, or weird. But our curiosity about other people can lead to wonderful conversations, to learning, to connection and to the chance to boost your success.

In *Anatomy of a Breakthrough* (2023), Adam Alter uses the example of TV's longest-running science fiction show, *Doctor Who*, to explore whether creative teams benefit from working with a cohesive and like-minded group or whether there is benefit in diversity and flux. As a programme that has run for six decades, it is perhaps not surprising that *Doctor Who* has attracted attention from researchers looking at team dynamics.

Gathering a broad data set, the researchers explored team make-up, collaboration, audience response, etc. Using the term 'network non-redundancy', they asked whether creative teams thrive more when there were new members of the team or when their network was closed, working with trusted and familiar teams. The findings were clear: creatives benefitted from the input of new talent and ideas. Network non-redundancy or novelty brought breakthroughs and 'periods of creative rejuvenation' (Alter, 2023).

Tube chat?

There seems to be an unwritten rule on the London Underground – the tube – that we do not talk to each other. In 2016, an American living in London for 20 years decided to launch an initiative to encourage conversations on the tube. Jonathan Dunne was fed up with the silence on his commute to London and guessed others might feel the same. He made 500 badges in the distinctive style of the London Underground with the words 'Tube chat?'.

He hoped to start a movement to get people talking as he handed out the free badges. The response was unexpected and not positive; in fact, people were horrified by the interruption. Badges were created in opposition, such as 'Don't even think about talking to me' or 'Shut up'.

However, not all reaction was hostile. Some loved the idea and requested further badges. Dunne produced another 500 and as well as many conversations on the tube he has created a dialogue about the nature of informal exchanges with strangers.

The learning and connection that can be created during a humdrum journey to work can really enrich our lives. Sandstrom talks of lessons of geography, culture and alternative ways of thinking. We have so much to learn and teach each other; our networking can be informal and spontaneous as well as structured and planned.

Sandstrom regularly strikes up conversations on her commute and says that she has learned a lot from these interactions. Her learning has been about different places and cultures, but also the capacity she has to push herself, to embrace the discomfort of the conversational approach that leads to broader understanding and knowledge.

Introvert or extrovert?

We are social animals and need to interact with each other to live in society, to live and to grow. But there are different ways to socialize, and while some people are excited at the prospect of a room full of unfamiliar people, seeing opportunity and interest, others might feel intimidated and drained at the prospect.

For extroverts there is an energy generated in connecting with others. Embracing a room full of new people is a chance to explore and to connect. Being able to start new conversations, or bring others in who might feel more intimidated by the prospect of talking to strangers, means that they can be excellent networkers. Sometimes lazily stereotyped as over-talkative and attention-seeking, the extroverted personality is simply more at ease in situations that offer the opportunity to engage with others.

Introverts can learn to network. They might need a little more time to prepare to engage socially and to introduce buffers around these events to allow them time to restore themselves, but it does not mean that as an introvert you cannot be a highly successful network.

You can be true to yourself and manage interactions authentically. You might say 'I really want to connect with people in this field, but I do find large events challenging, it would be great to follow up one-to-one'. As Susan Cain's important work in this field has shown (2013), identifying as an introvert does not limit opportunities. There is space for diversity.

Friends

There is irony in the fact that we hold our friends dear and trust them with secrets, we choose them to share special moments with us, we laugh together, mourn together, try new things together; but they might be the worst people to act as our guide or thinking partner as we explore reinvention.

Friends like us as we are. They are deeply subjective. They know our good points and also our flaws; they are also often sensitive to our needs and the things we might find it difficult to hear. It is those things that are a bit sticky that we do need to hear if we are going to allow change to happen. If we have a habit of interrupting a conversation, or being repetitive, or wearing too much scent – these things can put people off building a new relationship with us. It is useful to have this feedback, to know how we come across, how we might be experienced. Even if it stings a little bit.

However, someone who connects to you without the label of 'friend', but in the capacity of someone in your network, who wants the best for you, can tell you:

> 'That is the third time you have interrupted me. Your enthusiasm is great, but it is disruptive to a really meaningful conversation.'
>
> 'I've heard that story several times, are you aware? Can you share something else?'
>
> 'Scent is very personal; your scent is rather overpowering and could mean people move away from you.'

This is not to say that friends cannot be a valuable part of your network. It is just worth bracketing a conversation about your future plans with an invitation to talk to you, with an open understanding that the love and history between you may get in the way.

Bracketing

Bracketing in photography is a technique where the photographer takes repeated shots of the same image, but using different camera settings. This provides multiple photographic interpretations of the same object.

Bracketing is also a therapeutic technique that allows the listener to set aside their own values and beliefs in order to listen to a client with their, not our own, values and ethics predominant. In other words, with a different image of the person in front of them. The concept of unconditional positive regard is relevant here, an expression popularized by the humanistic psychologist Carl Rogers. In this model of client-centred therapy a person can say whatever they wish, behave however they choose, and they will be accepted. So the listener can hold the person speaking with their values and priorities in mind when exploring the issue presented.

The interlocuter may find the idea of money as a priority to be morally abhorrent, yet we do not reveal this to a client whose ambition is to make lots of money. A client may have sailed close to the wind, following the letter but not the spirit of the law in a way that differs from our own moral code, yet we do not pass judgement. A client may not demonstrate behaviour that is as focused on environmental issues as our own actions. Such bracketing does not mean we cannot disclose our own thoughts, but we must do this in a way that does not restrict the person speaking from being open about their position.

In psychoanalysis, Wilfred Bion encouraged those working with patients and groups to embark on the relationship 'without memory, without desire'. Essentially, to be a blank canvas to those we are engaged with, ready to listen deeply. The suspension of judgement is espoused by Greek philosophy in the notion of *epoche*. This withholding of judgement is akin to bracketing, allowing a subject to be explored without the usual assumptions associated with the subject matter.

It seems a deeply relevant term for us as we explore how to reinvent ourselves, the etymology of *epoche* being 'the point marking the start of a new period in time'.

Attachment styles

John Bowlby, the British psychoanalyst, brought us attachment theory as a way of understanding the emotional bond between an infant and its caregiver (Bowlby, 1979). The need for a close emotional bond extends beyond the infant and childhood and is a key part of working life. If dysfunctional attachment patterns are formed early in life, this can impact on the way we bond and form relationships in our adult life.

There are four recognized attachment styles that we may predominantly identify with:

1 A secure attachment style means that you are able to form secure and loving relationships with others, able to easily trust and be trusted.
2 An anxious attachment style is associated with neediness and clingy behaviour, such as worrying when someone does not text back quickly enough or thinking that someone does not care about you.
3 An avoidant attachment style is marked by a fear of intimacy. Those with this attachment style are reluctant to get close to others; they doubt their needs can be met in a relationship.
4 A disorganized attachment style, also known as fearful–avoidant attachment, reflects behaviours that can swing between extremes of anxiousness and avoidance. This style is least well researched.

This is relevant to our exploration of networking. Healthy attachment behaviour patterns mean that close contact comes easily – there is an expectation of goodwill. But for other attachment styles, things are more complex. Dysfunctional behaviour can result from attachment disorders, so an anxious/avoidant individual, for example, may be terrified of intimacy and commitment, but also distrust anyone who tries to get close. Dysfunctional behaviour is likely to intensify in times of pressure. Those with high avoidant patterns will find relating to other people very difficult.

Manfred Kets de Vries, Professor at INSEAD, has contributed significantly to the application of psychoanalytic ideas to organizational life (2004, 2014). He describes attachment disorders as being tricky to change, 'like an elephant', but they can be modified. He urges leaders to face their inner demons and recognize that the way they deal with attachment issues will influence the way they deal with problems, at work and at home.

Acknowledging the problem is always the first step, then finding help and support to address your attachment style through coaching or therapy will help you trust and communicate appropriately.

The helping relationships

Under the banner of helping relationships come a variety of connections we form that can support us as we move towards our future selves. This book does not focus on therapeutic or counselling support, something that is hugely valuable and highly recommended. The important place of a therapeutic relationship is something you may already be engaged in, and there are excellent resources to turn to in order to find the right therapy support.

Therapy is sometimes seen as a place to 'fix' yourself. I disagree. I see it as a place of self-discovery and exploration. There are so many options, from single session cognitive behavioural therapy to many years of daily analysis, group therapy or trauma-informed therapy. If this is something that you wish to explore, do your research. As with the areas of the helping relationship we will consider here, it is important to find the right connection. Do not be afraid to explore options: have a chemistry call, a trial session, meet and consider if the connection is right for you before you make a firm decision.

There are therapeutic models that can help us understand the way we network and our interactions with others, such as family constellation therapy and internal family systems (IFS) therapy. We will explore the power of working with a coach, having a mentor or embracing a thinking partner as some examples of the helping relationships that can support your reinvention.

Whichever helping relationship you choose to embrace, you will find someone walking along beside you, offering you space to share and plan. Perhaps it will be space to focus on your purpose and redirection, or perhaps simply protected time away from the demands of your work and family; a space that is just for you.

Working with a coach

As a coaching psychologist and supervisor who spends much of my professional life engaged in coaching relationships, I must declare a bias for the value of this particular helping relationship. Within the contained and supportive space of a coaching session, there is room for a client to explore vulnerability, to say the things it might feel dangerous to say outside of that space, to test ideas and to check experiences with a trusted partner. It is also time when people can think and be listened to deeply.

Attending to what another person has to say, without the need for reciprocity or the workplace politics and dynamics, can be both creative and challenging, allowing thinking that is powerful. As Nancy Kline expresses in the seminal *Time to*

Think (1999), 'The quality of our attention determines the quality of other people's thinking'. A coach is there to attend to your words, to explore your thinking and at times to shake things up.

Working with a coach can be pleasurable, but the objective is not just time with someone nice. The work can be deeply challenging and mean that a client confronts difficult insights about themselves and the mismatch between their self-perception and how others experience them.

There are so many ways in which one can work with a coach. For some there is a transactional relationship: a client may decide that they want to achieve certain clearly identified goals and work with a coach as a means to help them get there.

This solution-focused approach can be highly effective if you need support as you move towards such a clearly defined, specified and desired outcome. This approach, however, will not be helpful if you do not have clarity about what it is you are hoping to achieve. If you have a sense of uncertainty, a niggling feeling that you want more from your work and your life but are not sure what it is exactly you want, a coach who works with you in a more psychodynamic way might be more helpful.

Other styles of coaching might help you to change behaviour – cognitive behavioural coaching, for example. Here you are looking at the here and now, dealing with the thoughts that impact your behaviour and developing strategies to address those thoughts to lead you to change your behaviour, using techniques we touched on in Chapter 5. Another effective way of coaching in the here and now is the Gestalt approach, an exercise using the empty chair technique that features at the end of this chapter.

But at the heart of any impactful coaching is the coaching relationship itself. It is less about the label and more about the connection between coach and client. I personally take a pragmatic pluralist approach, responding to a client's needs as they present themselves. That might mean some guidance and direction in building confidence before an event, or it might mean delving deeply into the past to find out why these feelings of insecurity are so persistent.

Working with a mentor

Another option would be to work with a mentor. Coaching and mentoring share many similar characteristics and there is a lot of overlap: the confidential, trusted relationship, the time to think away from the workplace.

The key difference is that the mentor is sought out for their experience, knowledge and sector expertise, whereas a coach does not necessarily need to disclose specialist knowledge. The mentor is there to guide and share knowledge and experience; the coach is there to listen and challenge.

Way before mentoring appeared in the workplace, it had its place in ancient thinking. In Greek mythology, in Homer's epic *The Odyssey*, Odysseus leaves to fight in the Trojan war and leaves his friend Mentor in charge of his son Telemachus. The goddess of wisdom, Athene, also steps in to guide and counsel Telemachus in his father's absence, thus leading the word 'mentor' to be associated with a wise person, sharing guidance and offering counsel. The three most important thinkers in ancient philosophy, Socrates, Plato and Aristotle, were also linked in a knowledge-sharing and supportive relationship. Socrates taught and mentored Plato, who in turn taught and mentored Aristotle.

The notion of having a mentor in the workplace is fairly well-known and broadly welcomed. Most would find the idea of a relationship that offered support and challenge with someone we trust who is more knowledgeable and experienced than us appealing. This might be because we are thinking about embracing a new position at work, or entering a new field which is different to our past experience, or we are setting up a business for the first time, or we are newly appointed as a CEO.

In the 1970s, mentoring gained recognition in the business world as having a valuable place in the development of executives. Mentors and mentees were studied in the 1980s by Kathy Kram, who has published extensively on the subject of mentoring (1985, 2007). As the field has grown, Kram reflects on the special impact a mentoring relationship can have in our lives: a safe place of challenge and growth, a place of mutual learning.

Work has changed dramatically over the last six decades. Expectations of the kinds of work we will do, how long we will stay in organizations and the variety of skills and knowledge that we will need to embrace has also changed the way we connect with our mentors.

Mentoring has evolved – it is no longer just a traditional relationship of senior-junior mentoring. We have peer-to-peer mentoring, reverse mentoring and group mentoring. It is a two-way relationship – yes, it is about sharing knowledge and expertise, but a mentor can expect to learn as much as they teach.

WHEN THE SELF-CONFESSED 'NAUGHTY BOY' TURNS MENTOR

Stormzy is an artist, philanthropist and activist. He is a mentor with a difference – not only is he creating opportunities for disadvantaged pupils; he is also driving social mobility by establishing a scholarship for young black students at Cambridge University.

The 'Stormzy effect' on the intake of black students at the prestigious university has been significant. This year he extended his support to a further 30 students, funding their university fees and sponsoring their living costs.

Stormzy says he wants 'to shine a light where I can, do something where I can'. He has been a beacon of hope; reluctant to be described as a role model, he says simply that he has a purpose (Sylvester, 2021).

Ninety-seven per cent of people who have a mentor say they are valuable, and 89 per cent of those who have been mentored say that they would go on to mentor others. This is a helping relationship that is a win/win for mentor and mentee.

A thinking partner

A thinking partner is different from a coaching relationship or having a mentor. It is a mutually beneficial relationship that allows two people to share ideas and to be tested in a supportive but challenging environment; a space to think things through and to test ideas as partners.

The difference in a thinking partnership is that the two individuals do not usually work in the same environment, nor are they necessarily from the same industry or profession, although they can be. It is a space to be creative and innovative.

We are not restricted to one thinking partner – you may have an array of people you turn to in order to explore different ideas. There are people in my world who help me think differently about a range of topics from the Anthropocene to the arts, from mindfulness to technology. Thinking partners that challenge power dynamics and colonialism. Space to confront our privilege and our unconscious bias; space to think differently.

As you go about your work and broader life, you may come across people who interest you. You may not agree with everything they say or feel that you are from the same background or way of thinking. But you are intrigued by and interested in them. You may wish to spend time with them exploring ideas, challenging each other's thinking. You might want to understand more about the creative process – how an artist views the world – or how they think about crisis, environmental concerns or global uncertainty. Talk to them, invite them to be your thinking partner.

If they decline, do not be deterred. There are many more who will say yes.

FROM GRANADA AND AFGHANISTAN TO MUSWELL HILL – THE EVOLUTION OF A THINKING PARTNER

I was at the International Society for the Psychoanalytic Study of Organizations conference in Granada, Spain, presenting a session on psychoanalytic observation through the medium of Rembrandt's *The Night Manager*. This is a conference that meets annually and is both inspiring and intimidating. Writers, thinkers and analysts that have been reference points for me throughout my career mingle.

On an evening tour of the Alhambra, I met a first-time attendee, Rachel Ellison. Rachel is a former BBC journalist, now an executive coach, who was presenting a paper on her experiences of leadership in war-torn countries. We bonded over the medieval architecture and agreed to attend each other's seminars. From there, we developed a mutual respect and interest in each other's work.

There is space for us to be creative and commercial, to unpick family and professional life, yet always anchored in psychoanalytic reflection. It is a thinking partnership that embraces a dazzling agenda of the unconscious at work, female leadership, money, online coaching, coaching internationally and the publication of books and ideas. It is a precious connection.

The power of feedback

Feedback can be an extraordinary gift. We can learn something about ourselves that impacts our performance, the success of our ventures, our relationships, and the broader impact of our work. To really transform, we need to include people in our networks who are willing to share their observations and thoughts about how we are making decisions and how we are behaving.

Feedback is a critical friend; not in the sense of a friend who complains about you, but rather a trusted person who lets you know when things could be done differently, when the end you have in mind might be better served by a different approach. Shahroo Izadi (2018) describes getting better at listening to feedback as a way of learning.

We have to be able to receive and acknowledge feedback. That means being in a state of relative security, in a 'good enough' state so that the feedback does not destroy us, feeling psychologically safe – for the person sharing the feedback and for the recipient of the message.

A 2023 study highlights the impact of emotion and motivation on the effectiveness of feedback. Understanding the feedback process depends on the stages of feedback, the affective precursors, concomitants and consequences of feedback (Fong and Schallert, 2023).

The research conducted used a framework that tackled the following five questions:

1 What does the feedback mean to me? Is there a sense of helpfulness in the message being shared? Is the feedback about something within our control, or is it related to that which is outside of our control? Being told we are too inexperienced, for example, without clarity about what steps need to be taken to develop that experience is not helpful. Being given specific and detailed feedback can be rewarding and an opportunity to change.

2 How do I feel about the feedback? Do I trust the messenger? Even if the feedback is hard to hear, can I recognize its value, or does the feedback feel unfair or like an attack? Allow yourself time to process the message you have been given. If you feel it is unwarranted or unfair, you may say so. You may also choose whether to listen or to ignore the message.

3 Can I improve from the feedback? What can I do differently as a result of the feedback I have been given? Can I develop my performance? Can I try new techniques? Can I adopt new ways of working to help me improve?

4 Do I want to improve from the feedback? Essentially, does this matter to me? If we are given feedback about how to present better, but presentation is not key to our job, then do we need to attend to the feedback – is it a priority? You need to make the decision as to whether the feedback is relevant to your performance and something that you want to address. Remember, you can always deal with areas for development at a later date if the time is not right now.

5 Am I supported by others or by the context in dealing with feedback? Is this feedback constructive and in the spirit of the values of the place I am working or my business? Is this a priority area for my clients or stakeholders? Are there people or resources I can access to allow me to make improvements based on this feedback?

So for the feedback experience to be optimized, attention needs to be given to three factors:

1 Is the giver of the feedback respected and considered to have the receiver's best interests in mind?

2 Is the receiver in a sufficiently psychologically strong place to receive the feedback and welcome the impact on the way they function?

3 Is the context appropriate – is the feedback being delivered in a private place at an appropriate time?

Inviting feedback

Letting it be known that you welcome feedback is a great start in gathering information about your performance and your areas of strength and potential development. This is a thread that will run through any helping relationship, be it coaching, a thinking partnership, therapy or mentoring.

When you start to network you are there to explore and learn, but you can also seek feedback. Explain you are looking for constructive feedback to support your future plans. Ask for

FIGURE 8.1   The topography of feedback

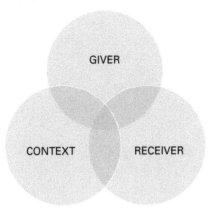

direct feedback. Be reasonable: don't share your 500-page manu-script, but do perhaps share a 200-word abstract and ask for comment. Or perhaps ask about your LinkedIn profile or your CV, the first impression you give, what you sound most passion-ate about.

We are all learners

The idea that we are all learners is important in the context of feedback. This is relevant for any sector or organization, but can feel particularly pronounced in medicine where feedback can have life-or-death consequences on a daily basis. Medical vision-aries like Atul Gwande and Henry Marsh have both spoken and written to the vital part open communication and the recogni-tion of human frailty plays in medicine.

For example, the vital importance of giving and receiving effective feedback in the field of pathology has been examined. Anyone working in this discipline be they trainees, profession-als, students, administrative assistants or fellows are integral to patient care.

Learning is at the heart of feedback, and feedback in medical education is important. Failure to provide feedback could be dire because... mistakes go uncorrected, good performance is not reinforced, and clinical competence is achieved empirically or not at all.

Jug et al, 2019

We learn by listening to people. To quote one of our reinvention stories, 'I will listen to anyone who has more knowledge than me'. This can mean the new recruit, the experienced executive or the intern.

In praise of an editor

Writing can be a deeply rewarding, stimulating and satisfying process. It can also be isolating, frustrating and generate a huge amount of self-doubt. We research, reflect and write in the hope that our words connect to the reader, that we have been able to communicate well. Sometimes that comes easily, and on other occasions it is painfully slow and unsuccessful.

An editor is another example of a helping relationship, someone who works alongside the writer, critiquing the work because, like the writer, they want to create the best experience for the reader. At times that means giving difficult-to-receive feedback. Words that have been carefully crafted are cut, ideas forestalled, errors identified. There are moments when it feels like there is a mirror being held up to you; you see your work in an altogether different way. It is perhaps not the image you intended – you have allowed your unconscious bias to leak out, you have betrayed your lack of confidence.

Yet as a result of the editing process, we see more clearly. We recognize that we have been lost in our own world and forgetting about the fundamental purpose of writing – for it to be meaningful to the reader. Having an editor is like a thinking partner, mentor and coach combined.

If only they were available in all walks of life.

Building your network, gaining new insights, knowledge and connections can be extremely helpful in your planning and steps towards reinvention. We should not overlook the pleasure and reciprocity of doing the same for others. We might have connections that our colleagues would find useful to meet; we might have knowledge and experience that would benefit our network.

The experience of giving back can be deeply rewarding; it might not offer a direct link to an opportunity for you, but it will enhance your reputation, allow you to do good and ultimately assist in another person's reinvention.

Online communities

We are part of a social phenomenon that involves more than a billion participants every day. This has a profound impact on the way we work together and the way we network (Williams, 2019). Over a lifetime, we develop a network of relationships and acquaintances that can support the way we live and work together; this is referred to as social capital.

The Office for National Statistics (ONS) defines social capital as 'the extent and nature of our connections with others and the collective attitudes and behaviours between people that support a well-functioning, close-knit society'. Your social capital will impact the way in which you access greater knowledge and opportunities. Availing yourself of online as well as in-person opportunities to build your network will greatly support your reinvention.

Research was conducted through a systematic review of peer-reviewed literature and conference papers to explore the use of online social networking sites, and the way these online communities can nurture an individual's meaningful connections. The findings confirmed that bonding social capital can be cultivated and nurtured by online social networking sites (Williams, 2019).

Many of us use social media to satisfy a need for relatedness. The impact of comparing ourselves unfavourably to beautifully curated images and profiles is one side of being present online. There is also the psychological benefit of receiving others' feedback, including reduced feelings of loneliness and higher social connectedness (Sun et al, 2023).

The global pandemic took much of our learning and networking online. Many of us who had rigidly believed that the online option was inferior or without merit had time to rethink these beliefs. The impact long-term on the absence of face-to-face social interaction while learning is still being investigated, but in the context of reinvention we have a magnificent resource available to us.

How to network online

This may feel comfortable to you and something you have grown used to over the last few years. It may feel like a natural environment to share ideas and connect with a global community. This is online networking at its best.

Yet some prefer the energy surrounding an in-person event, the chance to observe the way people are interacting, the opportunity to exchange eye contact and words that allow you to connect and to make an impression. There are also those people whose idea of networking brings to mind large events, warm glasses of wine in hand and a sea of faces, none of whom look welcoming or familiar.

Whatever your preference, online networking is here to stay, and is a place where there is so much potential for you to engage with interesting people, share ideas and test out your plans and ideas for reinvention.

You do not need to spend a lot of time developing content to post about your ideas or interests. This can come later as you develop confidence. At the start, just devoting a small amount of time every week to engaging online is a good first step. Many platforms can be extremely tempting to surf, and you can lose a great deal of time scrolling and exploring.

Set yourself a time limit and perhaps a target to comment on one or two posts a week, or to attend one event a month. When you do attend an online event, remember to introduce yourself in the chat; this is a gentle way to make yourself known to the world with your new identity or your desired future self.

Do whatever is manageable for you to allow you to explore what is out there, to discover what you can learn from.

Networking online for introverts

Introverts do need to work harder to network than those naturally extroverted individuals who are energized by a room full of people or who thrive with the opportunity to speak to lots of people in one go. Online networking provides containment for those who identify as introverts.

We learned from Gillian Sandstrom that introverts can learn to talk to strangers. The psychologist pushes herself to connect with 'weak ties' like strangers on the train to connect and to learn about life outside her experience.

If you are someone who gets depleted after a networking event, be that face to face or online, it is a good idea to take care of yourself. Allow time between networking to recharge your batteries. Limit the time that you are online. Prepare a few words of introduction and think in advance about some questions you may wish to ask.

Your profile

I have encountered many clients who are reluctant to present themselves as an authority in their field. They are concerned that they will be seen as exaggerating their expertise, or less worthy than other industry leaders or experts. The ideas we examined with the imposter phenomenon and the work that needs to be done on self-acceptance and self-compassion all collide in this act of presenting yourself to the world with your profile.

There are also those who claim to be world-leading experts when they are just at the start of their journey of discovery. You can be reserved about your achievements and ambitions, but still need to confront the way you present yourself to the world. You need to be clear and open about your strengths and what you wish to do with your future.

Because the first encounter someone will have with you is likely to be online, it is worth spending time on your online presence. Do an audit and cut what is out of date, and be clear about your ambitions, hopes and talents.

The words we choose to introduce ourselves with are important. We are complex creatures with multiple identities, but we also need to choose carefully where and how we reveal our vulnerability. I am not promoting insincerity, or a lack of candour, only a degree of caution in an untested environment. Once we are among those we respect and trust, we can reveal our vulnerabilities, safe in the knowledge that these will be welcomed as part of our whole selves.

Is your online photo up to date and in keeping with your ambitions? There is no right way to present yourself – it does not need to be formal or perfectly lit, just an indication of who you are. If you are not sure, ask a trusted advisor for their opinion.

Is the content in line with your ambitions? Are you listing the interests and topics that align with your hopes for your reinvention? You do not have to have copious content on your achievements, but an indication of what interests you.

Can you post content that places you as an expert in your field? Have you written any articles, posted any blogs or completed any interesting projects that you could share?

Internal networking

It might sound counterintuitive, but we may also need to do some internal networking. We are not always aligned in the way we integrate different parts of ourselves or the way we function in different systems and organizations. We explored the notion of inner voices, specifically our inner critic, earlier in the book, and this multiple narrative applies to our thinking around the way we manage our internal connections.

IFS therapy was developed by Richard Schwartz in the 1980s and is a therapeutic approach that looks at the different parts in a person's psyche (Schwartz and Morissette, 2021). Schwartz challenges the idea of a 'one-mind' view, and suggests we all have multiple personalities, or many sub-minds that interact with each other. Thinking involves different parts of ourselves talking to each other.

IFS therapy aims to bring harmony to these parts and to promote greater self-awareness and healing. So we may have different parts within us, each with its own emotions, beliefs and intentions. These can be clustered into three groups:

1 Managers – the protective parts that try to keep us safe and organize us.
2 Exiles – the injured parts of ourselves, those parts that typically experienced trauma.
3 Firefighters – the protection that puts out the emotional fire at any cost.

IFS therapy emphasizes the 'self' that can manage and lead different parts of themselves, recognizing our inner parts and knowing how to handle each one. This allows us to regulate our emotional reactions.

Another useful model to explore our inner dynamics is family constellation therapy, also called systemic constellations (Cohen, 2006). This looks at the hidden dynamics within a family system. It involves identifying and recognizing different family members and the way they function, in order to understand underlying issues about the way we interact and to facilitate healing. This can usefully be applied to our family of origin and previous generations. It can also be applied to our work groups.

The founder of this approach, Bert Hillinger, lived in South Africa for 16 years as a priest, where he studied traditional Zulu tribes, a society with a natural order to love, creating what he termed a healthy structure. He observed that at times issues from previous generations change the system, and that these issues are carried on through the generations. His theory taught that those who try to break free from family traditions are often labelled and rejected.

His work on the 'black sheep' of a family reflects his own life, a young German who rejected membership of the Hitler Youth Movement, then a priest who rejected the rigidity of the Catholic faith, later training as a psychotherapist. Here he brought the lessons from his observations of the Zulu into family constellation therapy – in particular the work that can usefully be done through the generations.

Intergenerational trauma is now recognized in formal scientific research (Cerdeña et al, 2021; Bombay et al, 2009).

Using techniques like psychodrama, where a person acts out a personal problem or conflict in a group context, or drawing, using objects to represent different members of the family (or work group) to encourage clients to identify patterns and relationships not previously considered, creating a matrix of information or a 'knowing field', Hillinger's method allows intergenerational healing; healing in yourself and in those around you.

This work can be intense, so is best conducted with a trained therapist so that emotions that emerge can be dealt with in a healthy way.

Exploring your opportunities

Some resistance to networking may come from a false narrative that says to network you must be insincere and sycophantic. You can network as your authentic self. You are in charge of the information you share and the questions you ask and answer. Building and nurturing relationships outside your immediate circle, with your 'weak ties', can improve the way you communicate your purpose but also open doors to learning and opportunity. There is evidence that it is through weak tie relationships that most new job opportunities arise, not through established business relationships.

Research exploring the different motivational focus of networkers distinguishes between those with a 'promotion' or 'prevention' mindset (Gino et al, 2016). Those with a promotion mindset have the benefits of networking in mind:

- growth
- advancements
- accomplishments

Those with a prevention mindset view networking as just something they must do for professional purposes. Carol Dweck's work on mindset has demonstrated our capacity to switch our mindset, so that we can move from prevention to promotion, albeit with some effort, changing our narrative from 'I absolutely hate networking events but have to go' to 'Perhaps it will be interesting, perhaps I will have an interesting conversation that leads to new opportunities' (Dweck, 2006, 2012).

Building your network helps build relationships. It can give you fresh ideas, open your eyes to different possibilities and even give you the chance to build long-lasting relationships and friendships. Through networking you can build your confidence and make contacts outside your immediate circle, beyond the echo chamber of the familiar.

We do not often hear people say 'I love networking!', but it is an important part of our identity, our working relationships and the potential to learn. It will form a vital part of your reinvention.

REINVENTION STORIES

An internal reinvention – to stay or go

Anita Banerjee was at a crossroads. After a decade in financial services, she came to coaching to explore whether she wanted to stay in an industry that did not always give her a sense of purpose. She liked her colleagues, was well remunerated and performed well. Her organization was sponsoring the coaching as she had been identified as a future senior leader.

Keen to please, she worked extremely hard and took criticism and any hint of negative feedback very badly. It made her feel like an imposter and an idiot.

Anita spoke of the guilt of her needs being potentially at odds with those of her organization. She came to coaching in a fragile state. Her father had recently been diagnosed with cancer, and her mother had died a few years before. In addition to her work, she was finding it hugely stressful caring for her dad.

Using compassion-focused coaching, her coach helped her to draw her lifeline with key ups and downs to recognize patterns in her life; to acknowledge her anger and her grief and her self-criticism, a reflection of the critical treatment she received from her father. As a child she was encouraged to be dutiful and respectful, and her needs were put last. The coaching offered her techniques to practise more self-compassion.

Anita gained insight into the other characters in her story, allowing her to validate and process difficult feelings. She was introduced to the idea of multiple selves and how her angry, anxious and ashamed parts had different ways of thinking, feeling and behaving.

At the end of the coaching Anita felt more forgiving of her father and more compassionate to herself. She decided not to move in the short term, but to work on her assertiveness and resilience, to welcome feedback but also to take better care of her wellbeing.

From East London bicycle delivery to flower fanatic and B Corp in Cornwall

Florence Kennedy set up her business, Petalon, delivering flowers to 50 London postcodes by herself on a bicycle. Now that she runs the only florist in Europe to achieve B Corp status, her aim is to do good alongside running her business, also certified carbon neutral.

Florence is self-taught and from the start was interested in sustainability, starting her journey by donating to the bee population in London for every bouquet sold. She learned on the job and by exploring other values-driven businesses, but ultimately the work was self-motivated – she and her team did it themselves.

Since moving to Cornwall three years ago, Petalon has transformed from a one-woman operation to delivering flowers nationwide, seven days a week. They are now able to offer 100 per cent Cornish-grown bouquets and have donated thousands of meals to the Cornish food bank.

EXERCISE

Your conversation challenge

Maybe you have a great circle of dear friends and colleagues whose company you really enjoy – a group where you belong. Or perhaps you are not well connected – maybe you are new to a location or someone who finds it hard to strike up connections.

Here is your conversation challenge – talk to someone new today:

- Find out something you didn't know!
- Think about how you might be different by knowing this.
- What were your pre-conversation predictions?
- What is your post-conversation experience?

EXERCISE

Building your network

As we have learned from this chapter, we can learn a great deal from those people not in our inner circle. I would encourage you to build your network and connect with people who you perhaps admire, but who are different from you. Start by reaching out to three people.

You do not need to set out a specific agenda, just that you would welcome the opportunity to broaden your horizons and learn from the person you have contacted. Do your research, let them know why you respect them.

Who are the people you look at with admiration? Who do you see has done things a bit differently? Who would you be most curious to find out more about? Perhaps there is someone who is in the industry you are keen to get into.

Ask them if they can spare 15 minutes for a Zoom call, or even a coffee in person. (And maybe you can ask them who else you should call?)

Ask them to keep you in mind. Be sure to follow up with a thank you.

Can you stay in touch?

EXERCISE

A trusted partner

Edgar H Schein emphasized the importance of working out your own career history and patterns of behaviour with someone else, a trusted partner. You should take it in turns to spend time exploring your talents, motives and values.

Answer the questions below (inspired by Shein) using 'never', 'sometimes', 'often' and 'always':

- I dream of being an expert in my field.
- I want to make a difference in the world.
- I will only feel successful if I am learning.
- I want to work flexibly and be free.
- I want to be in charge, a leader.
- I want to create a successful business.
- I need security and stability.
- I want to solve problems.
- I dream of creating something myself.
- I want to be challenged.

Contrast and compare your responses with a thinking partner – someone who you can be open and vulnerable with. By discussing your preferences with one another, you'll discover where your priorities lie and how they differ from others'.

EXERCISE

The movies of our lives

In trying to understand pleasing patterns in our relationships, psychotherapist Emma Reed Turrell (2021) outlines a therapeutic technique of imagining one's life as a movie. This technique is often used in EMDR (eye movement desensitization and reprocessing) therapy.

Negative statements that accompany you, flashbacks or distressing events are made into a movie to create distance, reprocessing the event and reimagining your experience more compassionately.

To create the movie of your life, imagine yourself in a movie theatre. Look at a big screen, and create the film of your life with other characters playing your part.

Imagine what happened to you happening to someone else. Notice how you feel about the person in the picture. Notice any negative cognition about yourself – you are being stupid, bad or defective.

Now, note your compassion for the character in the film. How does it feel in your body?

'I wish that person wasn't suffering, even if they made a mistake.' Bring compassion to mind – apply this to yourself.

When you create your movie script can you:

- notice any repeat storylines?
- identify the characters that accompany you?
- explore the outcomes that seem inevitable?

Have there been characters there for a short time yet impacted you?

What could the sequel to this movie look like?

EXERCISE

The empty chair exercise – DIY

The empty chair exercise was popularized by Fritz Perls, one of the founders of Gestalt therapy. Gestalt therapy emphasizes personal responsibility and works in the moment, the here and now.

The empty chair is a powerful exercise that allows you to connect to the 'other'. This might be an actual person; someone you are engaged with and have issues you wish to understand better; they could be from your past or in your life now. They do not need to be physically present. Or you may wish to use this exercise with the 'other' that is part of you – your critical voice, your future self or indeed any part of yourself:

1 Find a quiet space to work uninterrupted.
2 Place two chairs facing each other.
3 Sit in one of the chairs.
4 Invite the other (person or part of yourself) to sit in the empty chair.
5 Speak to the empty chair: explain how you feel, your thoughts and unresolved emotion. Take your time.
6 Now move to the empty chair and take up the role of the 'other'. Respond to what has been said.
7 You can move between chairs to continue the dialogue.

Using your imagination, you can converse with your chosen other as if they were present. It can help you see the situation from a different perspective, to gain deeper insight into your feelings and behaviour. It can also help to make abstract thoughts more concrete, to see things more clearly.

When working with a therapist, you may be guided through this process to help you express yourself and gain insight into your thoughts and emotions. Doing this exercise solo requires you to do that processing yourself; to think about what emerged, what needs further action and exploration.

Closing thoughts

This book was written at a time of great uncertainty in the world. A few years ago, we emerged from the 'great global pause' of the pandemic that caused many of us to stop and reflect on what we really wanted from our lives. There have been increasing environmental disasters and a reluctant acceptance of the age of the Anthropocene. Nations have been at war, our world economies have teetered, people's standards of living have suffered.

At a time of such unrest and disaster it can feel futile to think about your own plans, yet there is always hope. Humanity's memory of disaster, atrocities and collapse is short – we forget, we repeat, we go on. In this precious life we have been given we have the chance to make the most of what is available to us, to develop ourselves, to find our purpose, to make a difference, to grow; and for many that will mean reinventing ourselves.

This book has given you a chance to pause and think. To reflect on the cycle of your working life, to confront the endings and closures you will inevitably face and to plan for your next steps. We have explored the neuroscience behind reinvention and the encouraging capability of our brain to transform itself. We have delved into the meaning of age and the false restrictions we impose on ourselves because of our biological age.

Not every reinvention will be a resounding success. We may try numerous times before we land on the satisfying reinvention we are seeking. For every failure there is something to learn, and we can be certain that we are unlikely to rest in one place for too long. Life is about continuous reinvention.

Throughout we have drawn on psychological ideas to help us overcome obstacles and to thrive. I have encouraged you to be self-compassionate and use the many stories and exercises in the book to support your reinvention. You are not alone and there are people out there to walk alongside you, so build your tribe.

In Adam Phillip's book *Missing Out* (2013), he explores the amount of time we spend thinking about the lives we have not lived, the opportunities we have not taken and the parallel lives that might have been. We regret and resent our failure to be the person we wanted to be. We are, as Phillips describes 'haunted by the myth of our potential'.

This book is a way of changing the narrative of your life. Rather than facing the loss of what you didn't attempt, what you didn't embrace, what you didn't explore, use this book to help you attempt to embrace and explore new opportunities.

Do not strive for originality.

This may feel paradoxical – surely you should seek to do something fresh and unique? Many people reject the idea of following a path because it has already been taken by someone else. Perhaps that someone else has done it very well.

But this should not deter us. There is so much capacity to build on ideas, to take a tangent, to make things our own with our particular passion and style. I remember my initial disappointment at discovering there was a piece of research exploring mourning around the time of the financial crisis, just as I was finishing my PhD thesis on mourning and melancholia in the City of London. I was guided to welcome this; it showed that I was on to something interesting. People were curious about endings, and my original research would add to that narrative. This is a common thread in academic research.

So many businesses and endeavours are inspired by existing ideas and offerings. The way we communicate and network, the way we develop products, the way technology is developed, the way we design and market – every element of working life draws on already existing knowledge and expertise.

On transience

I have always loved Freud's 1916 essay 'On Transience', not just because it is short. It beautifully captures the value of being in the moment, the inevitability of death, the importance of appreciating the natural world around you, of recognizing that life is fleeting and needs to be embraced. That even with temporal limitation, we can still value short experiences and moments of wonder.

Freud wrote this paper at a time when the world was in flux. Two of his sons were fighting in the First World War, and Freud was particularly eloquent about the beauty of life, despite its transience. His writing was inspired by a walk in a forest with a young poet bereft at the prospect of the loss of beauty in the flourishing summer landscape that would soon die away:

> The value of all that is beautiful and perfect is determined only by its significance for our emotional lives: it does not need to survive and is therefore independent of the absolute duration of time.

His paper ends with the hope that lost objects will be replaced with new and possibly even more precious objects even after the losses of war. Objects in this context are not just things, but could be people or things that represent a person or part of a person. There is hope that life will be rebuilt and be enduring.

So we may be inspired by this sentiment when we think of what will be left behind as we embrace our new identity, our new job, our new way of being. It remains part of what made us who we are, that phase, that learning, those experiences brought us to now, to our current reinvention. One that may evolve again and again.

Future unknown

When we reflect on our lives and actions, we can see how we have changed, what we have learned, the mistakes we have made, the things that have gone wrong, the ways we have developed. There is a paradox that we look forward to the future and always expect our future life to be similar to the present... even when at the same time we look back and recognize just how much has changed.

The future is not only unknown, it is unknowable. A few decades ago, we could not have anticipated the changes in the way we work and live. Prior to the pandemic we would not have predicted the seismic shift in our working patterns or our advancement in working remotely and digitally. The numerous cultural, political and environmental changes we have witnessed would have been impossible to contemplate a decade ago.

Would we have conceived of a comic actor becoming the leader of a great nation? Of a teenager transforming and leading the global conversation about the environment? That technology would allow us to perform delicate heart operations?

Relating to your future self

If you do not connect to the real sense of your future self, you disconnect from the consequences of your actions. Almost as if you are dealing with an outsider, rather than someone you care about.

Research by Hal Hershfield (2023) has found that it can be deeply difficult to connect to our 'future selves'; that on a neural level we relate to our future selves as if they were a stranger. His research showed people how they might look in the future. Using virtual reality, participants faced a mirror. Staring back was either a digital image of themselves as they were in real time, or an image of them as their age-progressed selves. When tested later, those exposed to age-enhanced images expressed more concern for their future self.

Seeing themselves as older people connected participants to the person they would become, somebody older and with different needs than in their current situation. This was far more marked than a simple description of your older self. Identifying with that older person, they were more likely to do things that would benefit them, like planning for their future financial security.

We find ways of helping and supporting those we love and care about. If we think about our future selves as strangers, we are more likely to engage in a phenomenon known as temporal discounting. This occurs when we value an immediate gain over longer-term future gains.

Try to connect to the social, emotional and material gains you might require in the future. Where you are now is temporary. Perhaps you are single and will be in a relationship; perhaps you will become a parent or a grandparent; perhaps you will want to live in another country or start a business. All these different versions of yourself require thought and attention.

A warmer and closer relationship with our future self can take us to a place of self-compassion and empathy with our reinvented selves. It can also help us plan better.

Not yet

Carol Dweck has contributed substantially to the mindset movement. She has led an understanding that we can change the way we approach difficult circumstances by adopting a growth mindset and shown us the limitations of a fixed mindset.

She talks about a moment in her early career where she encountered a school where students who had failed a test were not graded as 'fail', but as 'not yet'. These students were being rewarded for effort, progress, engagement and perseverance. The words 'not yet' gave students confidence and a sense of possibility in the future.

This lesson is one we can take beyond the classroom. A growth mindset with thinking steeped in 'not yet' rather than 'not possible' shows us that achievement is attainable with the right attitude.

And now we come to the end. We have explored the importance of change not being linear; that it is rarely predictable and often iterative. I hope you have had time to reflect on who you are and your future self. I also hope you can be appreciative of who you are now, of all your skills, talents, flaws, learning and potential.

Reinvention is not a once-in-a-lifetime event. We are constantly evolving, so do not be despondent if your first attempt fails. Reflect and see what you learned; try something else.

So this might be the end of this book, but every chapter is there for you to refer back to. Use your imagination, be kind to yourself, appreciate your gifts and connections, be creative about what comes next. This author believes in your reinvention and will be cheering you on.

EXERCISE

A letter from you

This is the final exercise of the book. I invite you to both write a letter to your future self, and then, later, to reply to the letter from the future.

Research (Hershfield, 2023) shows that this dialogue with your future self helps avoid temporal discounting – that you begin to think about what decisions today will mean for you tomorrow and in a few years' time.

First, write a letter beginning 'Dear future self…'. Date the page.

In this letter, write to yourself about your plans for the future. Remember that when you are planning ahead, small steps are most likely to be achieved, so write of your cumulative small achievements that will help you reach your hoped-for future self:

- What are you curious about?
- What do you need to learn; what do you need to find out more about? Who will help you get that extra understanding and insight?
- Where do you need courage?
- What are you worried about – what part of the future is most concerning to you? Name your fears.
- What will make it worthwhile?
- Who do you admire around you? Who can you turn to for support and guidance? What is it about their values that speaks to you?
- What are the things that matter most to you?
- What are you grateful for? Although you have plans for your future self, there will be things you are grateful for in the present – personal qualities, people, opportunities, etc.

Now write a letter back from your future self. This will encourage you to take responsibility for your future self, forcing you to step into your own shoes further down the line.

Think about the things that have benefitted you, and what you have been most appreciative of. It will allow you to connect with you in the future.

References

Akhlaghi, F (2022) Transformative experience and the right to revelatory autonomy, *Analysis* 83 (1), 3–12

Allen, D G, Peltokorpi, V and Rubenstein, A L (2016) When 'embedded' means 'stuck': Moderating effects of job embeddedness in adverse work environments, *Journal of Applied Psychology*, 101 (12), 1670

Alma, D and Amiel, K (eds) (2020) *These Are The Hands: Poems from the heart of the NHS*, Fair Acre Press, Shropshire

Alter, A (2023) *Anatomy of a Breakthrough*, Heligo Books, Sweden

Anderson, K, Brien, K, McNamara, G, O'Hara, J and McIsaac, D (2011) Reluctant leaders: Why are some capable leaders not interested in the principalship? *International Journal of Management in Education*, 5 (4), 384–400

Armstrong, D (2018) *Organization in the Mind: Psychoanalysis, group relations and organizational consultancy*, Routledge, London

Bandura, A (2000) Self-efficacy: The foundation of agency, *Control of human behavior, mental processes and consciousness: Essays in honor of the 60th birthday of August Flammer*, 16

Banks, A P and Gamblin, D (2022) Successful everyday decision making: Combining attributes and associates, *Judgment and Decision Making*, 17 (6), 1, 255–86

Barhate, B and Dirani, K M (2022) Career aspirations of generation Z: a systematic literature review, *European Journal of Training and Development*, 46 (1/2), 139–57

Baumeister, R F and Leary, M R (2017) The need to belong: Desire for interpersonal attachments as a fundamental human motivation, *Interpersonal Development*, 57–89

Beckett, S and Duthuit, G (1949) Three dialogues, *Transition*, 49

Berg, J M, Dutton, J E and Wrzesniewski, A (2013) Job crafting and meaningful work. In B J Dik, Z S Byrne and M F Steger (eds), *Purpose and meaning in the workplace* (81–104), American Psychological Association

Berlin, I (1953) *The Hedgehog and the Fox*, Weidenfeld & Nicholson, London

Bickerstaff, I (2023) Meet Keir Starmer's heir apparent: Keir Mather, the new Gen Z MP, dubbed the 'Baby of the House', *Tatler*, www.tatler.com/article/who-is-keir-mather-labour-gen-z-mp-selby-and-ainsty (archived at https://perma.cc/G2MP-GBZ2)

Bolton, M J (2020) *Hello, Neighbor: Carl and Fred Rogers and a Process of Person-centered Mentorship*, Abrams Books, New York

Bombay, A, Matheson, K and Anisman, H (2009) Intergenerational trauma: Convergence of multiple processes among First Nations peoples in Canada, *International Journal of Indigenous Health*, 5 (3), 6–47

Boothby, E J, Cooney, G, Sandstrom, G M and Clark, M S (2018) The liking gap in conversations: Do people like us more than we think? *Psychological Science*, 29 (11), 1742–56

Bowlby, J (1979) The Bowlby Ainsworth attachment theory, *Behavioral and Brain Sciences*, 2 (4), 637–38

Brann, A (2022) *Neuroscience for Coaches: How coaches and managers can use the latest insights to benefit clients and teams*, Kogan Page, London

Bravata, D M, Watts, S A, Keefer, A L, Madhusudhan, D K, Taylor, K T, Clark, D M, Nelson, R S, Cokley, K O and Hagg, H K (2020) Prevalence, predictors and treatment of impostor syndrome: a systematic review, *Journal of General Internal Medicine*, 35, 1252–75

Buckland, F (2023) *Find your own path: How to create the life you really want*, Michael Joseph, Penguin Random House, Dublin

Buetler, K A, Penalver-Andres, J, Özen, Ö, Ferriroli, L, Müri, R M, Cazzoli, D and Marchal-Crespo, L (2022) "Tricking the brain" using immersive virtual reality: modifying the self-perception over embodied avatar influences motor cortical excitability and action initiation, *Frontiers in Human Neuroscience*, 15, 787487

Burns, D D (1989) *The Feeling Good Handbook: Using the new mood therapy in everyday life*, William Morrow and Co, New York

Burns, K M, Burns, N R and Ward, L (2016) Confidence—More a personality or ability trait? It depends on how it is measured: A comparison of young and older adults, *Frontiers in Psychology*, 7, 518

Butler, J (2004) *Precarious Life: The powers of mourning and violence*, Verso, Brooklyn, NY

Cain, S (2013) *Quiet: The power of introverts in a world that can't stop talking*, Crown, New York

Cerdeña, J P, Rivera, L M and Spak, J M (2021) Intergenerational trauma in Latinxs: A scoping review, *Social Science & Medicine*, 270, 113, 662

Cieciuch, J and Topolewska, E (2017) Circumplex of identity formation modes: A proposal for the integration of identity constructs developed in the Erikson–Marcia tradition, *Self and Identity*, 16 (1), 37–61

Clance, P R and Imes, S A (1978) The imposter phenomenon in high achieving women: Dynamics and therapeutic intervention, *Psychotherapy: Theory, Research and Practice*, 15 (3), 241

Clear, J (2018) *Atomic Habits: An easy and proven way to build good habits and break bad ones*, Cornerstone Press, Penguin, UK

Cohen, D B (2006) "Family constellations": An innovative systemic phenomenological group process from Germany, *The Family Journal*, 14 (3), 226–33

Cokley, K, Awad, G, Smith, L, Jackson, S, Awosogba, O, Hurst, A, Stone, S, Blondeau, L and Roberts, D (2015) The roles of gender stigma consciousness, impostor phenomenon and academic self-concept in the academic outcomes of women and men, *Sex Roles*, 73, 414–426.

Cokley, K, Smith, L, Bernard, D, Hurst, A, Jackson, S, Stone, S, Awosogba, O, Saucer, C, Bailey, M and Roberts, D (2017) Impostor feelings as a moderator and mediator of the relationship between perceived discrimination and mental health among racial/ethnic minority college students, *Journal of Counselling Psychology*, 64 (2), 141

Cokley, K, Stone, S, Krueger, N, Bailey, M, Garba, R and Hurst, A (2018) Self-esteem as a mediator of the link between perfectionism and the impostor phenomenon, *Personality and Individual Differences*, 135, 292–97

Collins, J (2001) *Good to Great*, Random House Business Books, London

Cozolino, L (2017) *The Neuroscience of Psychotherapy: Healing the social brain* (Norton Series on Interpersonal Neurobiology), WW Norton & Company, New York

Damasio, A R and Damasio, H, eds (2012) *Neurobiology of Decision-Making*, Springer Science & Business Media, Berlin

Davis, V (2022) *Finding Me*, Harper Collins, New York

Day, E (2019) *How to Fail: Everything I've learned from things going wrong*, Fourth Estate, London

De Botton, A (2001) *The Consolations of Philosophy*, Penguin, London

Didion, J (1968) On keeping a notebook, in *Slouching Towards Bethlehem*, New York: Farrar, Straus and Giroux

Doidge, N (2007) *The Brain That Changes Itself: Stories of personal triumph from the frontiers of brain science*, Viking Press, New York

Dryden, W (1999) *How to Accept Yourself*, Sheldon Press, London

Duckworth, A (2016) *Grit: The power of passion and perseverance*, New York: Scribner

Duke, A (2022) *Quit: The power of knowing when to walk away*, Penguin, London

Dunbar, R I and Shultz, S (2007) Understanding primate brain evolution, *Philosophical Transactions of the Royal Society, B: Biological Sciences*, 362 (1480), 649–58

Dunning, D (2011) The Dunning–Kruger effect: On being ignorant of one's own ignorance, *Advances in Experimental Social Psychology*, 44, 247–96

Dweck, C S (2006) *Mindset: The new psychology of success*, Random House, London

Dweck, C S (2012) Implicit theories, *Handbook of Theories of Social Psychology*, 2, 43–61

Eckert, P (2017) Age as a sociolinguistic variable. In *The Handbook of Sociolinguistics*, 151–67

Edmondson, A C (2018) *The Fearless Organization: Creating psychological safety in the workplace for learning, innovation and growth*, John Wiley & Sons, New York

Erikson, E (1959) *Identity and the life cycle*, International Universities Press, New York

Eskreis-Winkler, L and Fishbach, A (2019) Not learning from failure— The greatest failure of all, *Psychological Science*, 30 (12), 1, 733–44

Fong, C J and Schallert, D L (2023) "Feedback to the future": Advancing motivational and emotional perspectives in feedback research, *Educational Psychologist*, 58 (3), 146–61

Freud, S (1915) 'Those Wrecked by Success', in Some character types met with in psychoanalytic work, *Standard Edition*, 14, 309–33, Hogarth Press, London

Freud, S (1916) On Transience, *Standard Edition*, 14, 303–307, Hogarth Press, London

Friedman, D, Pizarro, R, Or-Berkers, K, Neyret, S, Pan, X and Slater, M (2014) A method for generating an illusion of backwards time travel using immersive virtual reality—an exploratory study, *Frontiers in Psychology*, 5, 943

Frost, R (1915) *North of Boston*, Henry Holt, New York

Future of Humanity Institute (nd) www.fhi.ox.ac.uk (archived at https://perma.cc/2DPB-SZSF)

Gerhardt, M W and Irving, P (2023) HBR Glassdoor 2019 D&I study

Gerhardt, S (2004) *Why Love Matters: How affection shapes a baby's brain*, Brunner-Routledge, New York

Gerhardt, S, Jowell, T and Stewart-Brown, S (2011) You don't talk about love in government, *Soundings*, 48, 145–157

Gignac, G E and Zajenkowski, M (2019) People tend to overestimate their romantic partner's intelligence even more than their own, *Intelligence*, 73, 41–51

Gilovich, T and Medvec, V H (1995) The experience of regret: What, when and why, *Psychological Review*, 102 (2), 379–95

Gino, F, Kouchaki, M and Casciaro, T (2016) Learn to love networking, Harvard Business Review, https://hbr.org/2016/05/learn-to-love-networking (archived at https://perma.cc/W525-G3VZ)

Goldman Sachs (2023) AI investment forecast to approach $200 billion globally by 2025, 1 Aug, www.goldmansachs.com/intelligence/pages/ai-investment-forecast-to-approach-200-billion-globally-by-2025.html (archived at https://perma.cc/GJ6P-LARZ)

Goodwin, B and Miller, K (2013) Research says, *Educational Leadership*, 70, 80–82

Grant, A (2021) *Think again: The power of knowing what you don't know*, Penguin, London

Grant, A M and Ashford, S J (2008) The dynamics of proactivity at work, *Research in Organizational Behavior*, 28, 3–34

Hablitz, L M and Nedergaard, M (2021) The glymphatic system: A novel component of fundamental neurobiology, *Journal of Neuroscience*, 41, (37), 7698–7711

Haidt, J (2006) *The Happiness Hypothesis: Finding modern truth in ancient wisdom*, Basic Books, New York

Hanson, R (2018) *Resilient: Find your inner strength*, Penguin, London

Harari, Y N (2014) *Sapiens: A brief history of humankind*, Random House, London

Harvard Business Review (2023) *Multigenerational Workplace: The insights you need*, Harvard Business Review Press

Haushofer, J (2016) CV of Failures, www.princeton.edu/haushofer/
Johannes_Haushofer_CV_of_Failures.pdf (archived at https://perma.
cc/6MBD-YCDG)

Hershfield, H (2023) *Your Future Self: How to make tomorrow better
today*, Piatkus, Great Britain

Hewitt, P L and Flett, G L (1991) Perfectionism in the self and social
contexts: Conceptualization, assessment and association with psycho-
pathology, *Journal of Personality and Social Psychology*, 60 (3), 456

Hidden Brain (nd) How Others See You (feat. Erica Boothby), https://
hiddenbrain.org/podcast/mind-reading-how-others-see-you/ (archived
at https://perma.cc/4NUN-7DK7)

Ibarra, H (2004) *Working identity: Unconventional strategies for reinventing your career*, Harvard Business Press, USA

Izadi, S (2018) *The Kindness Method*, Bluebird Books for Life, London

James, W (1892) *Principles of Psychology*, Macmillan, New York

Jarldorn, M and Gatwiri, K (2022) Shaking off the imposter syndrome: Our
place in the resistance. In *The Palgrave Handbook of Imposter Syndrome
in Higher Education*, Cham: Springer International Publishing

Jarvis, M A and Baloyi, O B (2020) Scaffolding in reflective journaling:
A means to develop higher order thinking skills in undergraduate
learners, *International Journal of Africa Nursing Sciences*, 12, 100195

Jug, R, Jiang, X S and Bean, S M (2019) Giving and receiving effective
feedback: A review article and how-to guide, *Archives of Pathology
and Laboratory Medicine*, 143 (2), 244–50

Kahn, S (2017) *Death & the City: On loss, mourning and melancholia at
work*, Karnac, London

Kahn, S (2019) *Bounce Back: How to fail fast and be resilient at work*,
Kogan Page, London

Kahneman, D (2011) *Thinking, Fast and Slow*, New York: Farrar, Straus
and Giroux

Kahneman, D and Tversky, A (1982) The psychology of preferences,
Scientific American, 246, 160–73

Katie, B (2007) *Question Your Thinking, Change the World: Quotations
from Byron Katie*, Hay House, Inc, Carlsbad, CA

Kellaway, L (2017) I became a teacher at 57. I am learning the hard
way – it is brutal, says Lucy Kellaway, *The Times*, www.thetimes.co.uk/
article/i-became-a-teacher-at-57-i-am-learning-the-hard-way-it-is-brutal-
gl69n3lxc (archived at https://perma.cc/R5LU-U7GC)

Kets de Vries, M F (2004) Organizations on the Couch: A clinical perspective on organizational dynamics, *European Management Journal*, 22 (2), 183–200

Kets de Vries, M F (2014) The group coaching conundrum, *International Journal of Evidence Based Coaching and Mentoring*, 12 (1), 79–91

Kimball, G (2017) *Ageism in Youth Studies: Generation maligned*, Cambridge Scholars Publishing, Cambridge

Klein, T, Kendall, B and Tougas, T (2019) Changing brains, changing lives: Researching the lived experience of individuals practicing self-directed neuroplasticity, St Catherine University, sophia.stkate.edu/ma_hhs/20 (archived at https://perma.cc/6DTR-3DJ7)

Kline, N (1999) *Time to Think: Listening to ignite the human mind*, Cassell Illustrated, London

Kline, N (2015) *More Time to Think: The power of independent thinking*, Cassell Illustrated, London

Klingsieck, K B (2013) Procrastination: When good things don't come to those who wait, *European Psychologist*, 18, 24–34

Kram, K and Ragins, B R (2007) *The Handbook of Mentoring at Work: Theory, research and practice*, Sage Publications, Thousand Oaks, CA

Kram, K E (1985) Improving the mentoring process, *Training & Development Journal*, 39 (4), 40–43

Kram, K E and Isabella, L A (1985) Mentoring alternatives: the role of peer relationships in career development, *Academy of Management Journal*, 28 (1), 110–32

Langer, E J and Roth, J (1975) Heads I win, tails it's chance: The illusion of control as a function of the sequence of outcomes in a purely chance task, *Journal of Personality and Social Psychology*, 32 (6), 951–55

Lent, R W and Brown, S D (2020) Career decision making, fast and slow: Toward an integrative model of intervention for sustainable career choice, *Journal of Vocational Behavior*, 120, 103448

Levinson, H, Price, C, Munden, K, Mandl, H, and Solley, C (1962) *Men, Management, and Mental Health*, Harvard University Press, Cambridge, MA

Levy, B (2009) Stereotype embodiment: A psychosocial approach to aging, *Current Directions in Psychological Science*, 18 (6), 332–36

Levy, B R, Slade, M D, Chang, E S, Kannoth, S and Wang, S Y (2020) Ageism amplifies cost and prevalence of health conditions, *The Gerontologist*, 60 (1), 174–81

Lewin, K (1947) Frontiers in group dynamics: Concept, method and reality in social science; social equilibria and social change, *Human Relations*, 1 (1), 5–41

MacLean, P D (1990) *The Triune Brain in Evolution: Role in paleocerebral functions*, Springer, New York

Marcia, J E (1966) Development and validation of ego-identity status, *Journal of Personality and Social Psychology*, 3 (5), 551–58

McGilchrist, I (2019) *The Master and his Emissary: The divided brain and the making of the western world*, Yale University Press, New Haven, CT

Medline, A, Grissom, H, Guissé, N F, Kravets, V, Hobson, S, Samora, J B and Schenker, M (2022) From self-efficacy to imposter syndrome: the intrapersonal traits of surgeons, *JAAOS Global Research & Reviews*, 6 (4), e22

Medvec, V H, Madey, S F and Gilovich, T (1995) When less is more: counterfactual thinking and satisfaction among Olympic medalists, *Journal of Personality and Social Psychology*, 69 (4), 603–10

Mehta, R and Zhu, M (2012) Do the worst of times increase creativity? Scarcity vs. abundance psychology and creativity, *NA - Advances in Consumer Research*, 40, 58–61

Meyer, K and Willis, R (2019) Looking back to move forward: The value of reflexive journaling for novice researchers, *Journal of Gerontological Social Work*, 62 (5), 578–85

Milkman, K (2022) *How to Change: The science of getting to where you want to be*, Vermillion, London

Milkman, K L, Chugh, D and Bazerman, M H (2009) How can decision making be improved? *Perspectives on Psychological Science*, 4 (4), 379–83

Mischel, W and Ebbesen, E B (1970) Attention in delay of gratification, *Journal of Personality and Social Psychology*, 16 (2), 329–37

Mlodinow, L (2022) *Emotional: The new thinking about feelings*, Allen Lane, UK

Modell, A H (2003) *Imagination and the Meaningful Brain*, MIT Press, Cambridge, MA

Monteiro, S, Sherbino, J, Sibbald, M and Norman, G (2020) Critical thinking, biases and dual processing: The enduring myth of generalisable skills, *Medical Education*, 54 (1), 66–73

Moran, J (2020) *If You Should Fail: A book of solace*, Viking, UK

Nash, P, Taylor, T and Levy, B (2020) The intersectionality of ageism, *Innovation in Aging*, 4 (Suppl 1), 846

Neff, K (2003) Self-compassion: An alternative conceptualization of a healthy attitude toward oneself, *Self and Identity*, 2 (2), 85–101

NPR (2016) Tom Hanks Says Self-Doubt Is 'A High-Wire Act That We All Walk', www.npr.org/2016/04/26/475573489/tom-hanks (archived at https://perma.cc/FW9B-9GUA)

Obama, M (2018) *Becoming*, Viking Press, New York

O'Neill, B (2023) The trouble with Keir Mather, *The Spectator*, www.spectator.co.uk/article/the-trouble-with-keir-mather/ (archived at https://perma.cc/JF8Q-7X6X)

Oshman, M (2021) *What Would You Do if You Weren't Afraid?*, DK, London

Perry, J (2012) *The art of procrastination: A guide to effective dawdling, lollygagging, and postponing*, Workman Publishing, New York

Petriglieri, G (nd) LinkedIn post, www.linkedin.com/posts/gpetriglieri_leadership-podcast-love-activity-7084163634238517249-WOBf/ (archived at https://perma.cc/6V3R-VDV8)

Phillips, A (2013) *Missing Out: In praise of the unlived life*, Penguin, London

Pink, D (2022) *The Power of Regret: How looking backward moves us forward*, Canongate Books, Edinburgh

Pink, D (2023) Summary of our mini survey on regret, www.danpink.com/summary-of-our-mini-survey-on-regret/ (archived at https://perma.cc/93X6-M4MQ)

Poynton, R (2019) *Do Pause: You are not a to do list*, Do Book Company, London

Prat, C (2022) *The Neuroscience of You: How every brain is different and how to understand yours*, Penguin, London

Reed Turrell, E (2021) *Please Yourself: How to stop people-pleasing and transform the way you live*, Fourth Estate, London

Rhisiart, M, Störmer, E and Daheim, C (2017) From foresight to impact? The 2030 Future of Work scenarios, *Technological Forecasting and Social Change*, 124, 203–13

Riggio, R E, Chaleff, I and Lipman-Blumen, J (2008) *The Art of Followership*, Wiley, Hoboken, NJ

Roscigno, V J, Zheng, H and Crowley, M (2022) Workplace age discrimination and social-psychological well-being, *Society and Mental Health*, 12 (3), 195–214

Rosen, M (2005) *Michael Rosen's Sad Book*, Candlewick Press, Somerville, MA

Rosen, M (2021) *Many Different Kinds of Love: A story of life, death and the NHS*, Ebury, London

Rosenberg, S (2017) *Accessing the Power of the Vagus Nerve: Self-help for anxiety, depression, trauma and autism*, North Atlantic Books, California

Rosu-Finsen, A, Davies, M B, Amon, A, Wu, H, Sella, A, Michaelides, A and Salzmann, C G (2023) Medium-density amorphous ice, *Science*, 379 (6631), 474–78

Samuels, J (2017) *Grief Works: Stories of life*, Penguin, London

Samuels, J (2020) *This Too Shall Pass: Stories of change*, Penguin, London

Sandstrom, G M and Boothby, E J (2021) Why do people avoid talking to strangers? A mini meta-analysis of predicted fears and actual experiences talking to a stranger, *Self and Identity*, 20 (1), 47–71

Sandstrom, G M and Dunn, E W (2014) Social interactions and well-being: The surprising power of weak ties, *Personality and Social Psychology Bulletin,* 40 (7), 910–22

Savickas, M L (2020) Career construction theory and counseling model, *Career Development and Counseling: Putting theory and research to work*, 3, 165–200

Schein, E H (1996) Career anchors revisited: Implications for career development in the 21st century, *Academy of Management Perspectives*, 10 (4), 80–88

Schwartz, R C and Morissette, A (2021) *No Bad Parts*, Sounds True, Louiseville, CO

Sharot, T (2011) *The Optimism Bias: Why we're wired to look on the bright side*, Random House, New York

Simpson, M, Richardson, M and Zorn, T E (2012) A job, a dream or a trap? Multiple meanings for encore careers, *Work, Employment and Society*, 26 (3), 429–46

Solms, M (2021) *The Hidden Spring: A journey to the source of consciousness*, Profile Books, London

Stefan, M (2010) A CV of failures, *Nature*, 468 (7322), 467

Stoeber, J, Lalova, A V and Lumley, E J (2020) Perfectionism, (self-) compassion and subjective well-being: A mediation model, *Personality and Individual Differences*, 154, 109708

Sullivan, S E and Al Ariss, A (2021) Making sense of different perspectives on career transitions: A review and agenda for future research, *Human Resource Management Review*, 31 (1), 100727

Sun, P, Xing, L, Wu, J and Kou, Y (2023) Receiving feedback after posting status updates on social networking sites predicts lower loneliness: A mediated moderation model, *Applied Psychology: Health and Well-Being*, 15 (1), 97–114

Swart, T (2020) *The Source*, Penguin, London

Sylvester, R (2021) Stormzy: the rap star who funds Cambridge scholarships, *The Times*, www.thetimes.co.uk/article/stormzy-the-rap-star-who-funds-cambridge-scholarships-kkcxzp8dg (archived at https://perma.cc/KCS2-3VWW)

TED (2023) A 3-Step guide to believing in yourself: Sheryl Lee Ralph, https://ed.ted.com/lessons/a-3-step-guide-to-believing-in-yourself-sheryl-lee-ralph (archived at https://perma.cc/7ZAQ-NJFS)

Topping, M E and Kimmel, E B (1985) The imposter phenomenon: Feeling phony, *Academic Psychology Bulletin*, 7 (2), 213–26

Treanor, J (2023) Why Britain's absent army are returning to work, *The Sunday Times*, 15 July

Tresemer, D W (2012) *Fear of Success*, Springer Science & Business Media, Berlin

Trunnell, E P and Braza, J F (1995) Mindfulness in the workplace, *Journal of Health Education*, 26 (5), 285–91

Uwagba, O (2021) *We Need to Talk About Money*, Fourth Estate, Dublin

Van Gennep, A (2019) *The Rites of Passage*, University of Chicago Press, Chicago (Van Gennep 1909, *Les Rites de Passage*)

Ware, B (2012) *The Top Five Regrets of the Dying: A life transformed by the dearly departing*, Hay House Inc, Carlsbad, CA

Watts, A (2022) *Collage as a Creative Coaching Tool: A comprehensive resource for coaches and psychologists*, Taylor & Francis, Milton Park, Oxon

Waworuntu, E C, Kainde, S J and Mandagi, D W (2022) Work-life balance, job satisfaction and performance among Millennial and Gen Z employees: A systematic review, *Society*, 10 (2), 286–300

Williams, J R (2019) The use of online social networking sites to nurture and cultivate bonding social capital: A systematic review of the literature from 1997 to 2018, *New Media & Society*, 21 (11–12), 2710–29

Winnicott, D W (1971) *Playing and Reality*, Penguin, London

Winnicott, D W (1974) Fear of Breakdown, *International Review of Psycho-Analysis*, 1 (1–2), 103–07

Wiseman, L (2010) *Multipliers: How the best leaders make everyone smarter*, HarperBusiness, New York

Wong, K (2018) We're all afraid to talk about money. Here's how to break the taboo. *New York Times*, www.nytimes.com/2018/08/28/smarter-living/how-to-talk-about-money.html (archived at https://perma.cc/2793-ZM8Q)

Index

The index is filed in alphabetical, word-by-word order. Numbers in main headings are filed as spelt out in full; acronyms and 'Mc' are filed as presented. Page locators in *italics* denote information contained within a Table.

Looking for another book?

Explore our award-winning
books from global business
experts in General Business

Scan the code to browse

www.koganpage.com/general-
business

From the same author

"This book will have a profound impact on those who read it. Not just of coping, but of flourishing. Not just of managing risks, but of unbound creativity."
Nicola Mendelsohn CBE, VP EMEA, Facebook

BOUNCE BACK

HOW TO FAIL FAST AND BE RESILIENT AT WORK

SUSAN KAHN

ISBN: 9780749497361

www.koganpage.com